'Elizabeth Brooker's book of case studies provides further indications that attachment ruptures underlie severe forms of music performance anxiety. It is encouraging to observe that therapists are now seeing beyond the overt symptoms of performance anxiety to the core issues that promote faulty schemata. This revised focus directs practitioners to broaden their therapeutic pallets to include treatments such as EMDR and clinical hypnotherapy that directly address these core problematic factors.'

Professor Dianna Kenny, Professor of Psychology/Music,
The University of Sydney

'This book makes a strong case for the use of psychodynamic therapies in the treatment of performance anxiety across a range of domains including music, sports and public speaking. The concisely written reflective case studies, which are informed by years of therapeutic practice and underpinned by academic research, highlight the uniqueness of people's experiences with anxiety and the potential of cognitive hypnotherapy and EMDR as interventions. The book is a must read for researchers, practitioners and the general public who wish to understand more about the role of dynamic therapies in the treatment of anxiety.'

Dr Alinka Greasley, Associate Professor of Music Psychology,
University of Leeds

'A fascinating book providing an in-depth account of the effective use of hypnosis and EMDR to tackle music performance anxiety. Highly recommended reading for performers, teachers and therapists to enhance understanding of the anxiety condition and the revelatory results of the therapy, even after a few therapeutic sessions.'

Dr Renee Timmers, Reader in Music Psychology,
University of Sheffield

Transforming Performance Anxiety Treatment

Transforming Performance Anxiety Treatment: Using Cognitive Hypno-therapy and EMDR offers a much needed and different approach to this issue, using two psychodynamic therapies, which work to bring about rapid and long-lasting change.

Using nine reflective case studies, the author examines two little used interventions: cognitive hypnotherapy (CH) and eye movement desensitisation and reprocessing (EMDR). The basic theories of cognitive anxiety and the emotions that underpin this condition are explored. The principles and protocols of CH and EMDR are explained, and how these psychodynamic therapies are adapted to effect permanent change.

The first book to examine these treatments for this condition, *Transforming Performance Anxiety Treatment* will be of interest for practitioners and therapists in training, as well as educators, professionals, and therapists working within competitive sports.

Elizabeth Brooker is an experienced professional musician, qualified hypnotherapist, EMDR practitioner and neuro-linguistic programmer. She has an MA in Music Psychology from the University of Sheffield and a PhD doctorate from the University of Leeds where the focus of her research was reducing anxiety experienced in music performance.

Transforming Performance Anxiety Treatment

Using Cognitive Hypnotherapy and EMDR

Elizabeth Brooker

Routledge
Taylor & Francis Group

LONDON AND NEW YORK

First published 2019
by Routledge
2 Park Square, Milton Park, Abingdon, Oxfordshire OX14 4RN
52 Vanderbilt Avenue, New York, NY 10017

Routledge is an imprint of the Taylor & Francis Group, an informa business

First issued in paperback 2020

British Library Cataloguing in Publication Data
A catalogue record for this book is available from the British Library

Library of Congress Cataloging in Publication Data
A catalog record for this book has been requested

ISBN: 978-1-138-61493-2 (hbk)
ISBN: 978-0-367-60676-3 (pbk)

Typeset in Times New Roman
by Swales & Willis Ltd, Exeter, Devon, UK

For all my patients who have suffered from performance anxiety

They have inspired me to tell their stories

Contents

Figures, tables and appendices

Figure

Table

Appendices

Preface

The main focus of this book is on anxiety experienced in different social environments, in particular in the performance arena. It has been written to help those individuals who suffer from performance anxiety by drawing attention to therapies that have been scientifically proven to be very effective for alleviating this condition. The reader is introduced to a therapeutic approach that focuses on the unconscious mind and to the psychological aspects that underlie and heighten anxiety.

Performance anxiety in any domain can be a crippling experience, causing mental anguish as well as uncomfortable physical symptoms of anxiety which can impair performance. It is non-discriminatory, affecting both amateur and professional performers alike, at any age or level of expertise, and in the worst case scenario it can lead to individuals abandoning promising careers in their chosen field.

Over the last three to four decades a large amount of research and money has been directed into alleviating performance anxiety, and yet the problem still exists. The reader may wonder why this should be the case. Current research is dominated by investigations focusing on the role that the conscious mind plays in exacerbating anxiety (explicit memories, conscious thoughts and feelings). However, performance anxiety is a psychological condition and as such the causes can be deeply embedded in the unconscious mind.[1] Therefore therapies directed solely towards explicit processes may not be the most beneficial for this condition. Very little research has focused on therapies that target the unconscious mind which stores implicit or automated processes. These processes become activated (without conscious awareness) and are triggered by past memories of negative experiences. The use of therapies that primarily target implicit processes should therefore be extremely effective in bringing about positive therapeutic change.

This book introduces the reader to two therapies which use such processes for the alleviation of performance anxiety: cognitive hypnotherapy (CH) and eye movement desensitisation and reprocessing (EMDR).

My doctoral research focused on the psychological aspects of music performance anxiety (MPA) and the role that the conscious and unconscious mind plays in maintaining this state. The investigations gave scientific evidence of the beneficial and rapid effects of CH and EMDR (after only two therapy sessions) for alleviation of this condition, using a nomothetic approach (the study of groups of individuals).[2] Many scientific investigations adopt this method although valuable insight can be gained into the real-life experience of performance anxiety when an idiographic approach is adopted (the study of the individual's experience). This book adopts such an approach, giving qualitative, descriptive information on the debilitating experience of performance anxiety. It focuses on nine reflective case studies in three different domains – music, sport and anxiety in the workplace (presentations and meetings) – using CH and EMDR, therapeutic treatments that target deep-seated dysfunctional thoughts and memories of past experiences. A reflective study gives a more rounded picture on the therapy adopted giving an overview of treatment effects from the patient's and the therapist's perspective, and reflects and critiques the choice of treatment.

As a professional piano and singing teacher, music psychologist, and private practitioner of CH and EMDR, my personal background is highly relevant to the writing and development of this book. During my teaching career, which has spanned more than forty years, I have been aware of the detrimental effect that anxiety can have on performance and the consequence of this for musicians. I too have suffered from performance anxiety and can empathise with those that are afflicted with this debilitating condition. In my clinical practice as a therapist I am presented with an array of disorders, many of which appear to have anxiety as their root cause. As the therapist conducting the research and subsequently writing the case studies, my aim is to integrate my clinical experience with the current literature on this condition, my therapeutic interests being centred round the most effective and long-lasting interventions for the treatment of performance anxiety.

To help understand the problem, it is important to include personal accounts of the performance experience as these give more detail, sensitivity and insight on a personal level into the understanding of performance anxiety. Therefore the case studies begin with the individual's own words (their narrative), each containing an abbreviated description of the progression of treatment and therapeutic outcome. This gives insight into the process of therapy by exploring the internal thoughts, feelings and experiences of the individuals. The effects of therapy on subjective anxiety and the long-term effects of treatment are given as well as reflections on the suitability of the treatment administered from a research standpoint, giving comparisons with other treatment approaches currently used for this condition.

This book has been written to appeal to a wide readership. The case studies should give better understanding of performance anxiety and of the two therapies presented here for alleviation of this condition. It should be of interest to those readers who have first-hand knowledge of performance anxiety and are interested in learning of the experiences of others in a similar situation. The book is further designed for those readers who are fascinated by the psychological processes which underlie this phenomenon and are looking for deeper understanding of this condition. Full details of the references are therefore given to assist in this, and of course it is hoped that it might inspire further research in the field.

Organisation of the chapters

The book is divided into two parts. Part I (Chapters 1–3) gives valuable information about performance anxiety and why this condition exists, as well as an overview of CH and EMDR. The reader will find that the bibliography is fairly extensive here, the reason being that any book of this kind is a record of a journey through the literature on the subject. Part II concentrates wholly on the case studies. The book has been divided in this way to enable those readers who are mainly interested in the case studies to by-pass the earlier chapters if they so wish. However, the reader should bear in mind that Part I contains information which will help them understand more clearly the content of the case studies.

Part I

Chapter 1 reviews the background of anxiety per se and further explores performance anxiety, with its many complexities. The relevant psychological aspects of this problem are discussed, specifically the role that cognitive arousal, emotion and memories play in heightening anxiety. The most popular therapies currently adopted for the alleviation of performance anxiety are documented and the effectiveness of these discussed. This chapter argues that therapies focusing on the conscious mind may not be the most effective method of treatment for this debilitating problem and calls into question current thinking on treatment that focuses on the conscious mind.

Chapter 2 looks at the development of CH, tracing the cognitive and behavioural roots of this little researched therapy in the area of performance anxiety. A section is devoted to hypnosis, before looking at the use of hypnosis as an addition to therapy (termed cognitive hypnotherapy) and discussing the benefits of such an integrated approach for the treatment of negativity and emotional disorders. The background, protocols and procedures of CH are given examining the effects in clinical studies in various domains before focusing on their use in the field of performance anxiety.

Chapter 3 focuses on EMDR, a powerful technique used to treat a variety of conditions including anxiety-related issues and trauma. EMDR stimulates a safe, effective and rapid processing of disturbing experiences, allowing the patient to achieve rapid resolution of their problems. Traumatic memories and desensitisation are at the heart of this treatment which is discussed fully. Scientific evidence is given for the beneficial effects of EMDR in situations of high trauma: terrorist attacks, victims of war, the trauma of earthquake. Documentation is also given of studies showing the effectiveness of EMDR in eradicating performance anxiety. The theory and protocols of this therapy are also provided for those readers who would like information on the standard procedures of this treatment.

Part II

Chapter 4 reviews the method and procedure used in the case studies. It gives the reasons why the case study is such an important tool for evaluating performance anxiety, specifically the value of studying the real-life experience of the individual in these anxiety-driven situations. It describes briefly the method used when conducting the case studies. In eight instances the long-term effects of therapy are also given.

In the following case studies (Chapters 5–13), subjective quotes are included and have been italicised. These are taken from the individual narrative or story related by the patient to the therapist.

Chapters 5 and 6 introduce two participants, both advanced pianists, who took part in the PhD research I conducted into music performance anxiety (MPA). In Chapter 5 we are introduced to Jane, who relates her experiences, not only of MPA, but of Attention Deficit Hyperactivity Disorder (ADHD), from which she has suffered since her mid-teens (for more than five years) and which she felt was exacerbating her performance anxiety. Her treatment (EMDR) is documented in detail. After the first of two treatments Jane described her feelings: *I felt I'd been underneath a table for all of these years and now I'm above the table looking down upon it. I feel positive again, light and free . . . it feels like a detox.*

In Chapter 6 the focus is on Dan. It is important to include Dan's experiences in this book as during the research period he had been randomly allocated two sessions of CH for the alleviation of MPA. Dan had a negative view of hypnotherapy and had a fear of feeling 'out of control' (Dan's words), and doubted the therapeutic effectiveness. The result was a non-effective outcome. It is an example of why randomly allocated therapies may not necessarily be effective; the therapy needs to suit the client.

The case studies reviewed in the following chapters are of patients from the author's private practice who were suffering from performance anxiety in various domains.

Chapters 7 and 8 review cases of individuals who had only one treatment session to effect permanent change. Chapter 7 documents Mary's experience of MPA and her treatment, which was hypnotherapy. This was administered after careful consideration by the therapist of the most appropriate treatment for her and the therapeutic outcome can be contrasted with Dan's. Mary is an example of how a confident adult of mature years can be totally overwhelmed in a first piano examination and described the experience as follows: *I felt that I was on show and let myself down . . . it was one of the worst experiences of my life. I couldn't see the music properly, my hands and fingers were shaking and they didn't seem to belong to me.*

Chapter 8 focuses on Sarah, a clarinettist playing in a prestigious semi-professional orchestra who had been experiencing *huge performance anxiety for several years. . . . On some occasions I chickened out of playing completely and on others I was shaking uncontrollably and unable to give a good performance.* Sarah's single therapy session consisted of EMDR (targeting past traumas) followed by hypnotherapy.

In Chapter 9 we meet Rebecca whose story has similarities with Sarah's in that traumatic experiences from her past were having a negative impact on her singing in public performances and in examinations: *I had always felt very nervous when performing and always seemed to have the image of my father in the background; I felt that he was judging and criticising me and that I was letting myself down.* Rebecca required two separate sessions of therapy, however: EMDR in the first followed by CH in the second, which was designed to strengthen and enhance therapy outcome.

Chapters 10 and 11 focus primarily on anxiety in the sports arena, looking at one professional and one amateur equestrian. In Chapter 10 we meet Beth, a competent professional horsewoman who had been confident in the sports arena and had won several competitions. However, following a traumatic incident with a horse in a dressage competition she experienced severe performance anxiety when competing and was narrowly missing winning gold and silver medals. On entering the arena she had negative thoughts, and feelings of fear and of not being in control: *I knew in myself that I was a good horsewoman and was capable of winning first prizes, but negative thoughts were always at the forefront of my mind. It's now nine years since this initial experience but when I go into the arena I feel as if I'm looking inward and this is stopping me from achieving my goal.* This case is a classic example of how one traumatic incident can destroy self-belief in one's achievements and impacts negatively in all similar performance environments.

Chapter 11 illustrates that anxiety can be a complex learned condition[3] experienced in a variety of forms having both a psychological and physical effect on the body. Penny contacted me initially for chronic irritable bowel syndrome (IBS). This is a small part of her narration: *For the last 15–20 years I have suffered daily from IBS and it is ruling my life . . . I love horse riding and do this on a regular basis and take part in small competitions . . . I feel scared before these events anyway as I always want to achieve success and not let myself down, and having the IBS hanging over me makes me feel worse . . .* This is a very interesting and complex case, and illustrates how cognitive anxiety can have a chronic physical effect on the body. During the five therapy sessions that this patient was given, her experience of living with the daily symptoms of both physical and mental anxiety was clearly highlighted, giving valuable insight into how negative experiences from the past impact on the present: a case of how the mind affects the body.

Chapters 12 and 13 feature anxiety in the workplace, focusing on presentations, meetings and conferences. Chapter 12 documents the story of Craig, a confident individual in many areas of life but lacking confidence and self-belief in the work-place, particularly when having to give important presentations: *If something significant arises such as important meetings or a presentation that I would have to give with a critical audience then I start to panic. This has been happening over the last year or so after an important meeting with significant others where I just fell apart. I lost my train of thought and felt that I couldn't speak, my mind just went completely blank and I wanted the ground to open up and swallow me.* He is now fearful that at any important meetings or presentations he will experience similar feelings and will be unable to control or deal with this.

In Chapter 13 we meet Margaret, who contacted me after a recent important presentation went badly wrong. She was shortly due to give another and was afraid that she would have a recurrence of the earlier symptoms, which she found very frightening. Blurred vision, shaking/trembling, dry mouth and not being able to focus are all common symptoms experienced by individuals when suffering from performance anxiety: *I have been noticing that I am becoming really anxious during presentations, which is an important part of my work. I don't start to worry days before the presentation as I prepare well and know exactly how I want the presentation to go, it seems to be minutes before it starts I get different physical symptoms. My hands start to shake, and my stomach begins churning. When I start speaking my voice shakes and I can't seem to control my movements, I lose focus and go blank and my mouth feels really dry . . . I didn't know what was happening the first time my mouth went dry and my voice started to shake and this made me feel really anxious. When I was a teenager*

I did conference presentations and I presented at exhibitions, and had no symptoms then no matter how large the audience. I don't know why this is happening now but it's really distressing me. The symptoms that she has experienced are the classic symptoms of performance anxiety. When the underlying reasons for this occurrence are targeted and addressed, negative thoughts can be replaced with positive perceptions of the forthcoming performance experience.

Chapter 14 concludes with the implications drawn from conducting the case studies and the author's recommendations for global exposure in order to generate awareness of these therapies as effective fast-acting treatments for performance anxiety. It further considers the contributions that CH and EMDR make to current favoured therapies that are in vogue, and are currently adopted for performance anxiety.

References

1 Alladin, A. (2010). Evidence-based hypnotherapy for depression. *International Journal of Clinical and Experimental Hypnosis*, *58*(2), 165–185.
2 Brooker, E. (2018). Music performance anxiety: A clinical outcome study into the effects of cognitive hypnotherapy and eye movement desensitisation and reprocessing in advanced pianists. *Psychology of Music*, *46*(1), 107–124.
3 Izard, C.E. (1977). *Human emotions*. New York: Plenum Press.

Acknowledgements

I offer my sincere thanks and appreciation to all the individuals whose case studies are documented here, sharing with us their stories and experiences of performance anxiety. Without their permission it would not have been possible to write this book.

My thanks go to Dr Alinka Greasley, University of Leeds, UK, who first planted the seed and encouraged me to write this book.

Permission was granted by White Rose Etheses Online (WREO), University of Leeds, UK, for inclusion of the case studies reported in Chapters 5, 6 and 8.

Part I

Performance anxiety and the use of psychodynamic interventions

1 Exploring performance anxiety

Challenging the dogma of preferred therapies in current use

Performance anxiety is thought to be a type of social anxiety where individuals experience psychological discomfort in certain situations.[1] It is the arousal experienced when having to perform in front of an audience: the fear of being judged in a situation deemed to be threatening where individuals feel that they are on show or in the spotlight. A public performance of any kind may heighten the degree of anxiety experienced embracing a gamut of mental, emotional and physical feelings. The problem is widespread and is frequently reported in performance situations in various domains. In fact, well-known professionals have described having bouts of acute performance anxiety. In the field of music: Maria Callas, Luciano Pavarotti, Barbra Streisand, Adele, Michael Jackson and Carly Simon. Similarly, in stage and media performances: Sir Laurence Olivier, Peter O'Toole, Oprah Winfrey, Burt Reynolds, Johnny Depp, Emma Stone and Brooke Shields. And in sport: David Beckham, Pete Harnish (baseball) and Charlie Belijan (golf) all acknowledge that they have been afflicted with the condition.

What is cognitive anxiety?

A description of anxiety was given as early as the first century AD by Seneca, a Roman philosopher, who suggested that there are more things to alarm us than to harm us, and that we suffer more in apprehension than in reality.[2] Two thousand years later anxiety and its many complexities relating to the cognitive, emotional and behavioural aspects of human performance illustrate the wisdom of his words. Cognitive anxiety usually occurs when individuals feel that they are being scrutinised and anticipate that their behaviour will fall short of what is expected, experiencing a fear of not matching one's own or others' expectations leading to embarrassment and humiliation.[3]

Psychologists generally differentiate between two types of anxiety: trait and state. Trait anxiety is an individual's normal level of anxiety when in a non-threatening situation, and it has been suggested that it is influenced by genetics.[4] State anxiety, on the other hand, is a temporary condition which can change according to environmental situations and pressures. It is the anxiety that is experienced during a public performance and has been described as overestimating the severity of a feared event and underestimating the coping resources and rescue factors which could be adopted to help the situation.[5] However there is a relationship between the two anxiety states in that individuals with high trait anxiety will experience correspondingly high state anxiety in a situation they see as threatening.[6]

Self-focused negative attention on forthcoming events plays a key role in the conception and maintenance of anxiety.[7,8] In fact it is argued that cognitive anxiety is exacerbated through the interactions of fearful thoughts, arousal of the autonomic nervous system (ANS) and overt behavioural responses to a perceived threat.[9]

Arousal and performance

The ANS is the body's emergency system which becomes activated in response to external events and instigates arousal. The 'fight, flight or freeze' response prepares the body for appropriate action including the effects of increased adrenalin in the blood stream ensuring the enhancement of physical and psychological energies.[9] However, in a performance situation, arousal can exacerbate anxiety resulting in a variety of unpleasant symptoms which can have a detrimental effect on performance quality.[10] Over-arousal can generate physiological (increased heart rate) and somatic symptoms of anxiety (nausea, increased muscle tension, trembling/shaking, dry mouth, sweating and 'butterflies'.[11,12] When arousal interferes with performance, concentration is interrupted and memory blocks occur which impact negatively on performance.[13]

A number of different theories have been suggested regarding the degree of arousal appropriate in performance and it is argued that there is an individual zone of optimal functioning (IZOF).[14] It is further suggested that these levels vary for different individuals depending on their personality and characteristics.[15] When arousal is low to moderate, the individual's attention on the performance is greater; however focus decreases as the levels of arousal are raised.[16] Task mastery, the complexity of the task, peer pressure and audience effects are also factors that affect arousal in performance.[17,18] Compounding these factors cognitive appraisal of the situation also affects emotional behaviour; the problem is a complex one.

The cognitive/emotional connection

Anxiety has been defined as a complex (learned) emotion where fear is combined with other emotions such as anger, shame, guilt and excitement.

In fact when fear and anxiety are generated in a threatening environment emotion plays an integral part in the outcome of the situation.[19] Anxiety places an emotional burden on individuals and can be extremely disruptive,[20] and it is claimed that tendencies towards emotional instability significantly predispose performing artists to symptoms of panic in situations perceived as traumatic.[21] When an environment is thought to be threatening psychological problems may develop[22] leading to an emotional episode,[23] when the components of anxiety, physiological arousal, subjective feeling and dysfunctional behaviour interact.[24] Performance is said to be based on this complex set of interactions that operate in cognitive and emotional states.[25]

Highly relevant to the therapies adopted in the case studies documented in this book is that some cognitive components and emotional processing operate outside conscious awareness.[26] In fact it is argued that unconscious emotional processing can leave a negative memory trace connected to a similar experience, no longer consciously remembered, which will impact on the present-day experience. In other words forgotten negative experiences can have a direct effect on a future event. Let us consider the implication of this and the importance of memories when operating in a performance situation.

Memories, emotions and behaviour as contributors to anxiety

Research has shown that implicit processes (processes no longer in conscious awareness) sometimes referred to as automated mental processes, produce an automatic response[27] and can trigger latent patterns of thoughts, emotions and behaviour, resulting in a vicious cycle of non-helpful behaviour.[28] In fact memories and emotions of past events which are unconsciously perceived are highly pertinent to performance as subsequent behaviour can be affected[29] causing both physiological and psychological symptoms.[30]

As early as 1896 Freud observed that memories are not written down to be 'engraved' or to remain unchanged forever but can be altered by subsequent events and re-transcribed. He further observed that subjective events could take on an altered meaning years after they had occurred, and during and after treatment patients experienced altered subjective memories of those events. Memories of negative experiences or events changed and had new meaning. To be changed, however, he argued that memories had to be conscious and become the focus of conscious attention. Those memories not easily accessible to the conscious mind were 'relived' rather than 'remembered'.[31]

Recent scientific research argues that cognitive disorders can be thought of as malconnections between the various synaptic regions of the brain, and that maladaptive experiences or memories disassemble the connections; however these can be reassembled by positive experiences that establish change.[32] This has important implications for the recall of implicit memory and for the effectiveness of therapies that focus on automated processes, as during psychotherapy experiences and beliefs are highlighted and targeted, and negative perceptions altered. This gives the individual the opportunity to revisit and change the maladaptive memory as the underlying neuronal networks and associated memories can be re-transcribed and changed.[33]

Current therapies adopted for the treatment of performance anxiety

The literature strongly suggests that anxiety affecting cognitive processes is key to performance outcome,[10,34,35] and that behavioural and psychological responses are exacerbated by this condition, leading to different approaches in the field.[36] However the current effects of treatment for performance anxiety appear to be mixed.

There is little investigative evidence of the effects of the physically based and physiological treatments on performance anxiety (yoga, the Alexander Technique, bio-feedback and relaxation therapy) although there appear to be some positive outcomes in the reduction of anxiety in those cases that have been reported. Yet another approach used for alleviation of this condition is social/mental skills training. However, a drawback with all of the above therapies is the large number of sessions required to achieve a positive outcome. The meditative interventions may also have a beneficial effect on stress and general anxiety levels but the long-term nature of these treatments would seem to be a disadvantage. This is both time-consuming and costly, and could be the main weakness of the documented therapies.

Although some positive effects have been found using the cognitive-based therapies, anxiety conditions are complex with many different causes. Cognitive therapies focus on the conscious mind, the explicit presenting problems and physiological symptoms and can be effective in cases where there are no core psychological problems; however, depending on the nature of the condition these therapies are not effective where deep-seated problems exist. It is argued that focusing on the conscious mind as opposed to uncovering the deep-seated cause of the problem may not be the most effective method when presented with individuals with anxiety-based emotional conditions. In fact it has been found that therapies that are symptom-based may be effective at the time of treatment but can lead to re-emergence of these or different symptoms longitudinally.[37]

Recent evidence from clinical outcome studies into mood and anxiety have concluded that the failure of interventions to attend to the broader issues of the behavioural problem results in sub-optimal outcomes. It has been shown that although the treatment may be effective in addressing the symptoms, it does not result in substantial reductions, and individuals can be vulnerable to the emergence of these or other disorders. An approach which identifies not only the presenting symptoms but the psychopathology underlying the symptoms would appear to give the optimum results.[38]

Writing as a therapist I suggest that to effect positive long-lasting change a radical approach is needed, targeting the core problems by assessing both explicit processes in conscious awareness alongside implicit processes no longer in conscious awareness. In the treatment of anxiety the effect of psychodynamic psychotherapy has been shown to be equal to or more effective than cognitive therapy, particularly when longitudinal outcomes were examined.[39]

Psychodynamic psychotherapy

Psychodynamic psychotherapies target automated mental processes no longer in conscious awareness. The primary focus of the therapy session is on the expression and treatment of emotional conditions, particularly anxiety.[39,40] Emotions and fears are changed by psychodynamic therapies which treat the underlying root cause of the problem and not just the presenting symptoms.[41] It is argued that individuals are not always aware of the source of their fears.[19] Negative cognitions/memories and emotions should be brought into full conscious awareness in order to be addressed, and this is best achieved through dynamic psychotherapy.[42] The author's personal experience in therapeutic practice over several years supports this. Psychodynamic therapy focuses on emotional experiences and fear reactions and the positive changes that can be brought about in this area of treatment. It follows that the lynchpin of subjective emotional feelings may hinge on the extent and negativity of past memories, which may instigate and exacerbate performance anxiety.

Research demonstrates that physiological reaction patterns to emotion-inducing events are stored in memory.[43] When fears and maladaptive thoughts are targeted during an altered state of consciousness, these can be desensitised and reprocessed,[44] and in fact it is argued that a broad multi-dimensional approach to therapy is needed, as it seems that various psychological factors are the causation of anxiety and each needs to be addressed.[45] Investigations into non-conscious and conscious thought give new perspectives on the way that anxiety is perceived and generated, guiding appropriate treatment that targets the underlying causes of the problem.[44] However, there are few studies in the field of performance anxiety adopting methods which access both conscious and unconscious processes.

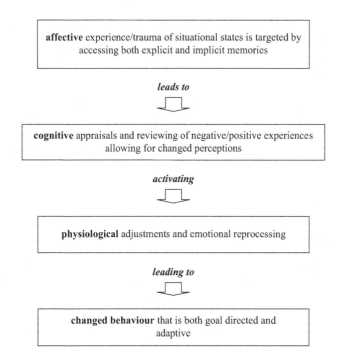

Figure 1.1 The four components of anxiety
Based on Miller and Chesky (2004)[46]

Both therapies adopted in the case studies documented here – cognitive hypnotherapy (CH) and eye movement desensitisation and reprocessing (EMDR) – focus on the role that such processes exert in exacerbating performance anxiety and are designed to desensitise and reprocess dysfunctional cognitions and memories. They follow identified principles based on four interrelated components of anxiety: affect, cognition, physiology and behaviour.[46] Figure 1.1 is based on these four components of anxiety and outlines how these factors are addressed during the application of CH and EMDR.

By adhering to these components the therapies address the cognitive, physiological and behavioural aspects of performance anxiety.

Summary

In this chapter it has been shown that performance anxiety is not straightforward but a complex, learned emotion, having components of fears and memories which exert a multitude of effects on performance. The importance of negative cognitions and the effect that these exert on emotions were highlighted, together with the importance of memories as contributors to anxiety. This chapter also explained that an array of therapies are being offered for the treatment of performance anxiety, but that few appear to offer any substantial change in this area and a large number of sessions are often required. It further noted that there is little research into the effectiveness of therapies that target automated mental processes (processes no longer in conscious awareness) and that this needs to be addressed.

Both interventions adopted in this book, CH and EMDR, have been chosen for the alleviation of performance anxiety as they focus on automated processes. Core problems are targeted, as well as the presenting symptoms, and should enable positive results to be achieved in a short space of time. These therapies can therefore be categorised as intensive short-term dynamic psychotherapies (ISTDP). CH works by accessing the unconscious mind while the patient is in a state of hypnosis, allowing changes in implicit memories; EMDR operates through bilateral stimulation, which induces a light trance enabling desensitisation of the fear memory trace.

Chapters 2 and 3 will give an overview of the dynamic psychotherapies adopted in the case studies reported here.

References

1 Crozier, W.R., & Alden, L.E. (2005). Constructs of social anxiety. In W.R. Crozier & L.E. Alden (eds), *Social anxiety for clinicians: The essential handbook* (pp. 1–26). Chichester: Wiley & Sons.

2 Wolfe, B.E. (2005). *Understanding and treating anxiety disorders: An integrative approach to healing the wounded self.* Washington, DC: American Psychological Association.

3 Wilson, G.D. (1997). Performance anxiety. In D.J. Hargreaves & A.C. North (eds), *The social psychology of music.* New York: Oxford University Press.

4 Cattell, R.B. (1973). *Personality and mood by questionnaire: A handbook of interpretive theory, psychometrics, and practical procedures.* San Francisco, CA: Jossey-Bass.

5 Beck, A.T., & Emery, G. with Greenberg, R. (1985). *Anxiety disorders and phobias: A cognitive perspective.* New York: Basic Books.

6 Spielberger, C.D., Gorsuch, R.L., & Lushene, R.E. (1977). S*tate–trait anxiety inventory for adults.* Palo Alto, CA: Consulting Psychologists Press.

7 Coles, M.E., Hart, T.A., & Heimberg, R.G. (2005). Cognitive-behavioral group treatment for social phobia. In W.R. Crozier & L.E. Alden (eds), *Social anxiety for clinicians: The essential handbook* (pp. 449–469). Chichester: Wiley & Sons.

8 Lewis, M. (2005). Origins of the self-conscious child. In W.R. Crozier & L.E. Alden (eds), *Social anxiety for clinicians: The essential handbook* (pp. 81–98). Chichester: Wiley & Sons.

9 Lang, P.J., Miller, G.A., & Levin, D. (1988). Anxiety and fear. In R.J. Davidson, G.E. Schwartz, & D. Shapiro (eds), *Consciousness and self-regulation* (pp. 123–151). New York: Plenum.

10 Fredrikson, M., & Gunnarsson, R. (1992). Psychobiology of stage fright. *Biological Psychology*, *33*, 51–61.

11 Friedman H.S., & Silver R.C. (eds) (2007). *Foundations of health psychology*. New York: Oxford University Press.

12 Powell, T.J., & Enright, S.J. (1990). *Anxiety and stress management*. London: Routledge.

13 Wilson, G.D., & Roland, D. (2002). Performance anxiety. In R. Parncutt & G.E. McPherson (eds), *The science and psychology of music performance: Creative strategies for teaching and learning* (pp. 47–61). New York: Oxford University Press.

14 Hanin, Y.L. (1986). State-trait anxiety research on sports in the USSR. In C.D. Spielberger & R. Diaz (eds), *Cross-cultural anxiety* (pp. 45–64). New York: Hemisphere Publishing Corp/Harper & Row Publishers.

15 Salmon, P.G. (1990). A psychological perspective on musical performance anxiety: A review of the literature. *Medical Problems of Performing Artists*, *5*(1), 2–11.

16 Mather, M., Mitchell, K.A., Raye, C.L., Novak, D.L., Greene, E.J., & Johnson, M.K. (2006). Emotional arousal can impair feature binding in working memory. *Journal of Cognitive Neuroscience*, *18*(4), 614–625.

17 Craske, M.G., & Craig, K.D. (1984). Music performance anxiety: The three systems model and self-efficacy theory. *Behaviour Research and Therapy*, *22*(3), 267–280.

18 Wilson, G.D. (2002). *Psychology for performing artists* (2nd edn). London: Whurr.

19 Izard, C.E. (1977). *Human emotions*. New York: Plenum Press.

20 Bishop, S.J. (2009). Trait anxiety and impoverished prefrontal control of attention. *Nature Neuroscience*, *12*(1), 92–98.

21 Marchant-Haycox, S.E., & Wilson, G.D. (1992). Personality and stress in performing artists. *Personality and Individual Differences*, *13*(10), 1061–1068.

22 Beck, A.T. (1964). Thinking and depression. Part II: Theory and therapy. *Archives of General Psychiatry*, *9*, 324–333.

23 LeDoux, J. (1993). Cognition versus emotion, again – this time in the brain: A response to Parrott and Schulkin. *Cognition and Emotion*, *7*(1), 61–64.

24 Scherer, K.R., & Zenter, M.R. (2001). Emotional effects of music: Production rules. In P.N. Juslin & J.A. Sloboda (eds), *Music and emotion: Theory and research* (pp. 361–392). New York: Oxford University Press.

25 Scherer, K.R. (1993). Neuroscience projections to current debates in emotion psychology. *Cognition and Emotion*, *7*, 1–41.

26 Lazarus, R.S., & Smith, C.A. (1988). Knowledge and appraisal in the cognition-emotion relationship. *Cognition and Emotion*, *2*, 281–300.

27 LeDoux, J. (1989). Cognitive-emotional interactions in the brain. *Cognition and Emotion*, *3*, 267–289.

28 Young, J.E., Klosko, J.S., & Weishaar, M. (2003). *Schema therapy: A practitioner's guide*. New York: Guilford Press.

29 Niedenthal, P.M., & Showers, C. (1991). The perception and processing of affective information and its influences on social judgement. In J.P. Forgas (ed.), *Emotion and social judgements* (pp. 125–143). Oxford: Pergamon Press.

30 Baddeley, A.D. (1999). *Essentials of human memory*. Hove: Psychology Press.

31 Freud, S. (1909/1957). Five Lectures on Psychoanalysis. In J. Strachey (ed. and trans.), *The standard edition of the complete psychological works of Sigmund Freud*, vol. *XI* (pp. 3–56). New York: W.W. Norton.

32 LeDoux, J. (2002). *The synaptic self: How our brains become who we are*. New York: Viking.

33 Doidge, N. (2008). *The brain that changes itself: Stories of personal triumph from the frontiers of brain science*. London: Penguin Books.

34 Beck, A.T. (1970). Cognitive therapy: Nature and relation to behaviour therapy. *Behavior Therapy*, *1*(2), 184–200.

35 Kirchner, J.M. (2003). A qualitative inquiry into musical performance anxiety. *Medical Problems of Performing Artists*, *18*, 78–82.

36 Andrade, J., Kavanagh, D., & Baddeley, A. (1997). Eye-movements and visual imagery: A working memory approach to the treatment of post-traumatic stress disorder. *British Journal of Clinical Psychology*, *36*, 209–223.

37 Paolino, T.J. (1981). *Psychoanalytical psychotherapy: Theory, techniques, therapeutic relationship, and treatability*. New York: Brunner/Mazel.

38 Brown, T.A., & Barlow, D.H. (2005). Dimensional versus categorical classification of mental disorders in the fifth edition of the Diagnostic and Statistical Manual of Mental Disorders and beyond: Comment on the special section. *Journal of Abnormal Psychology*, *114*(4), 551–556.

39 Shedler, J. (2010). The efficacy of psychodynamic psychotherapy. *American Psychologist*, *62*(2), 98–108.

40 Westen, D., & Morrison, K. (2001). A multidimensional meta-analysis of treatments for depression, panic, and generalized anxiety disorder: An empirical examination of the status of empirically supported techniques. *Journal of Consulting and Clinical Psychology*, *69*(6), 875–899.

41 Schwartz, J.M., & Begley, S. (2002). *The mind and the brain: Neuroplasticity and the power of mental force*. New York: Regan Books.

42 Alladin, A. (2010). Evidence-based hypnotherapy for depression. *International Journal of Clinical and Experimental Hypnosis*, *58*(2), 165–185.

43 Lang, P.J. (1979). A bio-informational theory of emotional imagery. *Psychophysiology*, *16*, 495–512.

44 Rossi, E.L., & Cheek, D.B. (1994). *Mind-body therapy: Methods of ideodynamic healing in hypnosis*. New York: W.W. Norton.

45 Alladin, A. (2008). *Cognitive hypnotherapy: An integrated approach to the treatment of emotional disorders*. Chichester: John Wiley & Sons.

46 Miller, S.R., & Chesky, K. (2004). The multidimensional anxiety theory: An assessment of and relationships between intensity and direction of cognitive anxiety, somatic anxiety, and self-confidence over multiple performance requirements among college music majors. *Medical Problems of Performing Artists*, *19*(1), 12–20.

2 Cognitive hypnotherapy

Changing negativity and anxiety

Cognitive hypnotherapy (CH) is an integrated approach for the treatment of emotional disorders, fusing hypnotic techniques with the protocols of the cognitive and behavioural therapies, offering an addition to therapy which strengthens the therapeutic outcome and facilitates the resolution of resistant symptoms. The integration of two disciplines gives added strength and impact for the maximum therapeutic effect, and was first used by Lazarus in 1973, when hypnotic techniques were incorporated into behavioural procedures.[1] The term 'cognitive hypnotherapy' was first coined in 1994, when Alladin adopted a multimodal approach for the treatment of depression, and it has been further used for the treatment of various other psychological conditions.[2,3] In fact it has been suggested that as a result of incorporating techniques from another approach into one's own main theoretical domain, the core ideas of the one are integrated into the latter (or 'host' theory), changing both and resulting in a new assimilative integrative model.[4]

Cognitive therapy

The idea of cognitive therapy took root in the late 1960s and early 1970s when Aaron Beck, an American psychiatrist, developed a treatment specifically for depression called 'cognitive therapy' when he identified tendencies in the personality likely to promote negative thinking. Positive thoughts, imagery and experiences were encouraged, leading to the alleviation of presenting symptoms.[5,6] Cognitive therapy based on Beck's generic formulation is organised around the idea that behaviour is based on schemas, core beliefs and assumptions, and that these are shaped by early experiences.[7] Schematic thoughts or schemas can be positive or negative, and consist of memories, attitudes, core beliefs and assumptions related to past experiences. These factors, if occurring in certain threatening circumstances, can result in individuals spiralling into negativity and consequential psychological problems.[7]

Cognitive theory emphasises the importance of underlying negative distortions of schemas, memories and core beliefs that produce automatic thoughts of failure and humiliation in the drive for perfection in an individual's performance.[6] The principles of cognitive theory were extended in the late 1970s when Lang proposed a three-system model of fear comprising three components of anxiety – cognitive, physiological and behavioural – which he suggested were interactive, yet partially independent.[8] These components of anxiety would become operational in a situation deemed to be threatening such as a public performance, or where an individual felt they were 'on show'. The theories and contributions of Beck and Lang have influenced the choice of therapies adopted in the author's case studies, as both CH and eye movement desensitisation and reprocessing (EMDR) address the principles advocated by these thinkers.

Behavioural therapy

Behavioural theory, in contrast to cognitive theory, is based on the premise that undesirable behaviours are learned and as such can be 'unlearned' through a process of systematic desensitisation.[9,10] Behavioural theorists consider that specific phobias and anxiety conditions are acquired through a process of classical conditioning, and that all learned responses derive from innate behavioural patterns, the stimulus/response paradigm.[11] As early as 1924 Watson argued that desired behaviours can be taught and reinforced and undesired behaviours eliminated. These ideas were expanded in the 1950s when Skinner suggested the theory of shaping behaviour by a system of rewards and punishment,[12] the behaviourists concentrating on systematic desensitisation and sequencing of negative images.[13]

Behavioural and cognitive theories, however, both focus on changing dysfunctional behaviour that occurs in feared situations and on positive visual imagery of the situation in which the maladaptive behaviour occurs. Other commonalities are management of physiological and somatic symptoms of anxiety and verbally assisted coping.

A distinction between the two approaches is that behavioural psychologists argue that conscious thoughts such as beliefs, plans and goals also influence behaviour and emotions, and as such can be changed positively through verbally accessible knowledge, whereas cognitive therapists target the patient's unhelpful reported thoughts. The methodologies of behavioural therapists were integrated with the cognitive techniques first introduced by Beck, resulting in techniques and procedures that distinguished between conscious beliefs and unconscious representations in memory.[14] This was a new concept developed from behavioural therapy which encouraged therapists to use techniques aimed at changing the negative/positive paradigm through the use of language and became known as cognitive behavioural therapy.

Cognitive behavioural therapy

For the purpose of this review the formulation devised by Persons is used,[15] as this is most usually associated with cognitive behavioural therapy (CBT), and bridges the gap between cognitive and behavioural formulations.[16] It focuses on negative experiences, which can lead to negative automatic thoughts and assumptions, and can be accompanied by feelings of dread, apprehension and fear of failure. Negative thoughts can result in dysfunctional emotions, behaviours and physiological and somatic symptoms of anxiety.[15]

The protocols and procedures adapted from Persons's formulation are used to treat psychological conditions, and enable development of flexible realistic beliefs. Individuals are helped in the pursuit of goals, and emotional problems are aided and overcome by directing cognitions towards memories, images, thoughts and attention. CBT focuses on the way individuals think and act in specific circumstances and how emotional and behavioural problems may be overcome.[17] However, although CBT appears to be the preferred treatment for anxiety-based conditions, no theory/therapeutic action is without flaws, and a number of issues have been identified with this approach:[18]

1   The failure to consider experiences in the past in relation to the present in generating anxiety.
2   The effective role that cognition plays on physiological symptoms in the body.
3   The failure to recognise the role of the unconscious mind in overt behaviour.
4   The failure to recognise that human thought and action are socially embedded.
5   Core problems are not treated.

In fact there is increasing concern regarding the relapse rate at follow-up sessions for those patients who have undergone symptom-based cognitive behavioural treatment,[19] and it has been argued that a large number of sessions are usually required and the effects are not long-lasting.[20] New cognitive models are now being developed considering the role of cognitions and emotions in generating anxiety, including a meta-cognitive model (MCM)[21] and an emotion dysregulation model (EDM).[22] However, neither of these models takes into account the role of the unconscious mind in the way that anxiety develops. The use of hypnosis allows access to the unconscious mind, and used as an adjunct to the cognitive behavioural techniques adds leverage to therapeutic outcome and can be used as a means of empowerment in new and creative ways.[23]

Hypnosis

Hypnosis itself is not a therapy; however, it provides a broad range of techniques that can easily be integrated into the cognitive behavioural approach and can be easily assimilated with many forms of therapy. It allows individuals to relax deeply so that a hypnotic trance state can be achieved. In fact trance is a special state where behaviour may be altered, enabling subjects to reassociate and reorganise inner psychological complexities.[24] While in trance the therapist aims to address the patient's unconscious mind, as during this state the critical faculty of the mind is bypassed. Selective thinking may be established with positive thoughts substituting former judgemental cognitions. This enables the processing of thoughts in the unconscious mind which are then transferred to the conscious in the waking state.[25] When patients are fully relaxed perceptions are changed quickly and positive subjective experiences occur replacing negative ones. In fact it is argued that rapid change in perceptions is attributed to the brisk and profound behavioural, emotional, cognitive and physiological changes brought about by hypnosis which appears to bring great comfort and relief.[26]

When hypnosis is added to a particular form of therapy whether behavioural, cognitive or cognitive behavioural therapy, the effects can enhance the treatment outcome.[27] The powerful treatment approach using hypnosis as an adjunct to therapy adds leverage to treatment, shortens treatment time and gives a quicker resolution of the unwanted condition.[28,29] In fact it has been suggested that by accessing the unconscious mind the process of hypnosis establishes positive cognitions which are then acted upon in the conscious state. It can be powerful in altering problem behaviours, dysfunctional cognitions and negative emotions.[30] Individuals are more highly motivated to engage with the therapist's requests while in the hypnotic state. This process of communication results in positive imaging, memory recall and suggestions for dealing with future stressful encounters (tools used in hypnotherapy). Muscle relaxation and focused breathing used in the hypnotic induction also contribute to the reduction of anxiety.

Two different types of hypnotherapy in current use are 'Ericksonian hypnotherapy' and the 'meta model'. Ericksonian philosophy emphasises the ability of individuals to access their own resources to improve the quality of their lives, recontextualising the memory, the effect of fear and physiological hyper-arousal. Accessing the unconscious mind through hypnotic suggestions strengthens the innate tendency of the mind to heal itself.[31]

In comparison the 'meta model', which can be termed 'conversational hypnosis', deals only with information available in conscious memory at the verbal level, and therefore does not access the unconscious mind.[32]

Ericksonian hypnotherapy has been chosen for use in the current case studies as this technique uses a set of procedures to alter the state of consciousness. During this state it has been suggested that the memory and meaning of negative experiences can be changed through emotional processing, as well as decreasing the somatic symptoms of anxiety associated with the event.[33-35]

Hypnosis as an adjunct to therapy: cognitive hypnotherapy

The potential benefits of an add-on hypnotherapy treatment and the efficacy of clinical hypnosis are well documented in the literature, with regard to conditions such as the following:

- PTSD;[36]
- headaches and migraines;[37]
- pain control and reduction in trauma re-experiences;[38]
- self-hypnosis during labour and childbirth;[39]
- hypertension;[40]
- sleep disorders;[41]
- irritable bowel syndrome;[42,43]
- diabetes (types 1 and 2).[44]

The above research reports that hypnotherapy appears to be psychologically beneficial for a number of wide-ranging conditions and warrants further investigations.

However, little research has been conducted using hypnotherapy as an intervention in the performance domain, and as the nine case studies documented in this book centre around performance anxiety, this section now looks at current research conducted into this condition using hypnotherapy as a treatment.

Two pilot studies using hypnotherapy were conducted with musicians suffering from performance anxiety,[45,46] and these were subsequently extended in a large-scale project with pianists. Using two groups, a hypnotherapy and a control group, it was found that the hypnotherapy group but not the control group showed a significant reduction in music performance anxiety (MPA) which was still evident six months later.[47] Further research was conducted into MPA for the alleviation of this condition using CH and EMDR (both interventions focus on automated mental processes). Forty-six advanced pianists were randomly assigned into groups:

treatment or control. Two groups received two therapy sessions of either CH or EMDR between two concerts; the third group was a non-treatment group and acted as the control. Both quantitative and qualitative data were collected throughout the research period. The results showed that both therapy groups (but not the control) experienced a significant reduction in state anxiety at a second performance post-intervention and a significant improvement in the quality of performance.[48]

Anxiety in public speaking was investigated testing the effect of CBT as a single therapy and CBT with the adjunct of hypnosis. It was found that although both treatments effectively reduced anxiety in performance, the addition of hypnosis to CBT generated expectancies among participants for greater change which further enhanced treatment effects and produced a faster drop in anxiety levels post-treatment.[49] In fact a meta-analysis investigating a wide variety of targeted disorders showed that the patients receiving CBT, where hypnosis was used as an adjunct to therapy, displayed a substantial improvement compared with 70% of the patients receiving only CBT. The finding that hypnosis added to CBT treatment produces a faster drop in anxiety levels after treatment is a particularly important finding for any forthcoming research into performance anxiety.[50] In a review of the empirical status of the use of hypnosis in conjunction with CBT programmes, it was concluded that existing studies demonstrate substantial benefits by the use of hypnosis as an adjunct to CBT.[51] One-dimensional procedures have their limitations; however a multimodal approach to treatment offers an effective alternative.

It can be argued, however, that as hypnosis influences behavioural and psychological responses it is difficult to assess whether a placebo effect is operative here; if it is, the extent to which it plays a role is also difficult to assess. For a number of patients hypnosis may act as a placebo due to positive expectations. There is evidence that hypnotic trance inductions are beneficial for those patients who believe in their efficacy,[52,53] and there is further evidence that patients' attitudes and beliefs can have a profound therapeutic effect in both medical and psychological conditions.[54] This effect may be difficult or impossible to control but if it enhances suggestibility and positive therapeutic outcome, then it can be beneficial and add to the impact and strength of the therapy.

Summary

This chapter has looked at the genesis of cognitive and behavioural therapies and the subsequent merging of these into CBT. The cognitive behavioural approach for the treatment of anxiety-based conditions was discussed and this was compared to the effectiveness of treatment when hypnosis is used as an adjunct to therapy. The studies reported in this chapter show that hypnotherapy as an added treatment to CBT brings positive change rapidly in cognition and physiology, impacting on subjective behaviour. This was shown in a number of domains including performance anxiety. Treatment using cognitive hypnotherapy is based on individual case formulation for various emotional problems including anxiety in performance. However the paucity of research investigating performance anxiety using therapies such as hypnotherapy that target the unconscious mind was noted, and further research in the field is required.

Chapter 3 reviews and evaluates EMDR, another dynamic, innovative and hypnotically based treatment for anxiety-based disorders. Both CH and EMDR are directed therapies that focus on negative emotions and memories, and by doing so free individuals from distressing symptoms and maladaptive patterns of thinking.

References

1 Lazarus, A.A. (1973). 'Hypnosis' as a facilitator in behaviour therapy. *International Journal of Clinical and Experimental Hypnosis, 6*, 83–89.
2 Gold, J.R., & Stricker, G. (2001). Relational psychoanalysis as a foundation for assimilative integration. *Journal of Psychotherapy Integration, 11*, 47–63.
3 Gold, J.R., & Stricker, G. (2006). Introduction: An overview of psychotherapy integration. In G. Stricker and J.R. Gold (eds), *A casebook of psychotherapy integration* (pp. 3–16). Washington, DC: American Psychological Association.
4 Messer, S. (1992). A critical examination of belief structures in integrative and eclectic psychotherapy. In J.C. Norcross & M.R. Goldfried (eds), *Handbook of psychotherapy integration* (pp. 130–168). New York: Basic Books.
5 Beck, A.T. (1967). *Depression: Clinical, experimental and theoretical aspects.* New York: Harper & Row.
6 Beck, A.T. (1970). Cognitive therapy: Nature and relation to behaviour therapy. *Behavior Therapy, 1*(2), 184–200.
7 Beck, A.T. (1964). Thinking and depression. Part II: Theory and therapy. *Archives of General Psychiatry, 9*, 324–333.
8 Lang, P.J. (1977). Imagery in therapy: An information processing and analysis of fear. *Behavior Therapy, 8*(5), 826–836.
9 Orman, E.K. (2003). Effect of virtual reality graded exposure on heart rate and self-reported anxiety levels of performing saxophonists. *Journal of Research in Music Education, 51*(4), 302–315.
10 Orman, E.K. (2004). Effect of virtual reality graded exposure on anxiety levels of performing musicians: A case study. *Journal of Music Therapy, 41*(1), 70–78.
11 Wolfe, B.E. (2005). *Understanding and treating anxiety disorders: An integrative approach to healing the wounded self.* Washington, DC: American Psychological Association.

12 Skinner, B.F. (1953). *Science and human behaviour*. New York: Macmillan.
13 Wolpe, J., & Lazarus, A.A. (1966). *Behavior therapy techniques: A guide to the treatment of neuroses*. New York: Pergamon Press.
14 Brewin, C.R. (1996). Theoretical foundations of cognitive behaviour therapy for anxiety and depression. *Annual Review of Psychology, 47*, 33–57.
15 Persons, J.B. (1989) *Cognitive therapy: A case formulation approach*. New York: W.W. Norton.
16 Wills, F. (2009). *Beck's cognitive therapy*. Hove: Routledge.
17 Alladin, A. (2008). *Cognitive hypnotherapy: An integrated approach to the treatment of emotional disorders*. Chichester: John Wiley & Sons.
18 Clark, A. (2008). *Supersizing the mind: Embodiment, action, and cognitive extension*. New York: Oxford University Press.
19 Paolino, T.J. (1981). *Psychoanalytical psychotherapy: Theory, techniques, therapeutic relationship, and treatability*. New York: Brunner/Mazel.
20 Kenny, D.T. (2011). *The psychology of music performance anxiety*. Oxford: Oxford University Press.
21 Wells, A. (2002). Worry, metacognition, and GAD: Nature, consequences, and treatment. *Journal of Cognitive Psychotherapy, 16*(2), 179–192.
22 Mennin, D.S., Heimberg, R.G., Turk, C.L., & Fresco, D.M. (2002). Applying an emotion regulation framework to integrative approaches to generalized anxiety disorder. *Clinical Psychology: Science and Practice, 9*, 85–90.
23 Alladin, A. (2010). Evidence-based hypnotherapy for depression. *International Journal of Clinical and Experimental Hypnosis, 58*(2), 165–185.
24 Barnett, E.A. (1989). *Analytical hypnotherapy: Principles and practice*. Glendale, CA: Westwood Publishing.
25 Rossi, E.L., & Cheek, D.B. (1994). *Mind-body therapy: Methods of ideodynamic healing in hypnosis*. New York: W.W. Norton.
26 DePiano, F.A., & Salzberg, H.C. (eds) (1986). *Clinical applications of hypnosis*. Norwood, NJ: Ablex.
27 Brown, D.P., & Fromm, E. (1986) *Hypnotherapy and behavioral medicine*. Hillsdale, NJ: Lawrence Erlbaum.
28 Dengrove, E. (1973). The use of hypnosis in behaviour therapy. *International Journal of Clinical and Experimental Hypnosis, 21*, 13–17.
29 Yapko, M.D. (2003). *Trancework: An introduction to the practice of clinical hypnosis* (3rd edn). New York: Brunner-Routledge.
30 Barrios, A.A. (1973). Posthypnotic suggestion in high-order conditioning: A methodological and experimental analysis. *International Journal of Clinical and Experimental Hypnosis, 21*, 32–50.
31 Erickson, M.H., & Rossi, E. (1974). Varieties of hypnotic amnesia. *American Journal of Clinical Hypnosis, 17*, 143–157.
32 Rossi, E.L., & Cheek, D.B. (1994). *Mind-body therapy: Methods of ideodynamic healing in hypnosis*. New York: W.W. Norton.
33 Bryant, R., Moulds, M.L., Guthrie, R., & Nixon, R. (2005). The additive benefit of hypnosis and cognitive-behavioral therapy in treating acute stress disorder. *Journal of Consulting and Clinical Psychology, 73*, 334–340.

34 Dozois, D.J.A., & Westra, H.A. (2004). The nature of anxiety and depression: Implications for prevention. In D.J.A. Dozois & K.S. Dobson (eds), *The prevention of anxiety and depression: Theory, research, and practice* (pp. 9–41). Washington, DC: American Psychological Association.

35 Spiegel, D., & Classen, C. (1995). Acute stress disorder. In G.O. Gabbard (ed.), *Treatments of psychiatric disorders* (vol. 2, pp. 1521–1535). Washington, DC: American Psychiatric Publishing.

36 Abramowitz, E.G., Barak, Y., Ben-Avi, I., & Knobler, H.Y. (2008). Hypnotherapy in the treatment of chronic combat-related PTSD patients suffering from insomnia: A randomised, Zolpidem-controlled clinical trial. *International Journal of Clinical and Experimental Hypnosis*, *56*(3), 270–280.

37 Hammond, D.C. (2007). Review of the efficacy of clinical hypnosis with headaches and migraines. *International Journal of Clinical and Experimental Hypnosis*, *55*, 207–219.

38 Shakibaei, F., Harandi, A.A., Gholamrezaei, A., Samoei, R., & Salehi, P. (2008). Hypnotherapy in management of pain and re-experiencing of trauma in burn patients. *International Journal of Clinical and Experimental Hypnosis*, *56*(2), 185–197.

39 Abbasi, M., Ghazi, F., Barlow-Harrison, A., Sheikhvatan, M., & Mohammadyan, F. (2009). The effect of hypnosis on pain relief during labor and childbirth in Iranian pregnant women. *International Journal of Clinical and Experimental Hypnosis*, *57*(2), 174–183.

40 Gay, M-C. (2007). Effectiveness of hypnosis in reducing mild essential hypertension: A one-year follow-up. *International Journal of Clinical and Experimental Hypnosis*, *55*(1), 67–83.

41 Graci, G.M., & Hardie, J.C. (2007). Evidence-based hypnotherapy for the management of sleep disorders. *International Journal of Clinical and Experimental Hypnosis*, *55*, 288–302.

42 Golden, W.L. (2007). Cognitive-behavioral hypnotherapy in the treatment of irritable-bowel syndrome-induced agoraphobia. *International Journal of Clinical and Experimental Hypnosis*, *55*(2), 131–146.

43 Keefer, L., & Keshavarzian, A. (2007). Feasibility and acceptability of gut-directed hypnosis on inflammatory bowel disease: A brief communication. *International Journal of Clinical and Experimental Hypnosis*, *55*(4), 457–466.

44 Xu, Y., & Cardena, E. (2008). Hypnosis as an adjunct therapy in the management of diabetes. *International Journal of Clinical and Experimental Hypnosis*, *56*(1), 63–92.

45 Plott, T.M. (1987). An investigation of the hypnotic treatment of music performance anxiety. Dissertation, University of Tennessee.

46 Stanton, H.E. (1993). Research note: Alleviation of performance anxiety through hypnotherapy. *Psychology of Music*, *21*, 78–82.

47 Stanton, H.E. (1994). Reduction of performance anxiety in music students. *Australian Psychologist*, *29*(2), 124–127.

48 Brooker, E. (2018). Music performance anxiety: A clinical outcome study into the effects of cognitive hypnotherapy and eye movement desensitisation and reprocessing in advanced pianists. *Psychology of Music*, *46*(1), 107–124.

49 Schoenberger, N.E., Kirsch, I., Gearan, P., Montgomery, G., & Pastyrmak, S. (1997). Hypnotic enhancement of a cognitive-behavioral treatment for public speaking anxiety. *Behavior Therapy, 28*, 127–140.
50 Kirsch, I., Montgomery, G., & Saperstein, G. (1995). Hypnosis as an adjunct to cognitive-behavioral psychotherapy: A meta-analysis. *Journal of Consulting and Clinical Psychology, 63*, 214–220.
51 Schoenberger, N.E. (2000). Research on hypnosis as an adjunct to cognitive-behavioral psychotherapy. *International Journal of Clinical and Experimental Hypnosis, 48*, 154–169.
52 Lazarus, A.A. (1973). 'Hypnosis' as a facilitator in behaviour therapy. *International Journal of Clinical and Experimental Hypnosis, 6*, 83–89.
53 Spanos, N.P., & Barber, T.X. (1974). Toward a convergence in hypnosis research. *American Psychologist, 29*, 500–511.
54 Harrington, A. (ed.) (1997). *The placebo effect*. Cambridge, MA: Harvard University Press.

3 Eye movement desensitisation and reprocessing

Transforming trauma and the emotional mind

Eye movement desensitisation and reprocessing (EMDR) is a relatively new psychotherapy having its inception in 1989 when it was introduced by Francine Shapiro, a senior research fellow at the Mental Institute in Palo Alto, California. It was primarily used in the treatment of Post-Traumatic Stress Disorder (PTSD); however, treatment protocols have evolved embracing other forms of trauma responsible for psychological and physiological disorders and it is now applied to an increasingly wide variety of problems, particularly those that are anxiety-based.

This innovative psychotherapy is rooted in behavioural theory (see Chapter 2, p. 13); however it adopted a new method of trauma treatment incorporating bilateral eye movements. Subsequently it was discovered that other forms of bilateral stimulation (tactile and auditory) also resulted in beneficial outcomes.[1,2] Through a process of desensitisation the treatment achieved positive changes in traumatic memories, as well as a reduction in anxiety. The philosophy underlying this approach to treatment is that individual conditions that are emotionally based can be healed quickly, effectively and profoundly; dissociative disorders, phobias, and the consequences of these and other past negative-rooted traumas can be changed and new behaviours emerge using EMDR.[3]

The expansion of EMDR

Over the last three decades the use of EMDR has expanded widely to include therapy covering a wide range of pathologies; it is now used in the treatment of trauma, anxiety disorders and associative conditions as well as phobias. In 2004 it was placed in the 'A' category as strongly recommended for the treatment of trauma and anxiety-related conditions by both the American Psychiatric Association and the American Department of Defense. Numerous studies have provided evidence for the effectiveness of this treatment for both category 'A' patients (the highest level of trauma, including threat of death) and experiences categorised as small or 't' trauma (anxiety conditions contributing to significant psychological distress requiring treatment).[4-8]

EMDR has evolved from a simple technique into an integrative psychotherapy that addresses both the cognitive perception of trauma and the resultant physiological condition, an interaction of mind and body. It is based on the premise that earlier life experiences can bring about a continued pattern of similar affect, behaviour and cognition, the three main constituents of anxiety, and that present day stimuli can elicit similar affective behavioural memories of earlier experiences.[9] It is believed that desensitisation and cognitive restructuring take place at a neuro-physiological level by means of adaptive processing used in EMDR. If the past event has been one of negativity or trauma an individual's behavioural response to the present day experience will be consistent with the affective responses of the past. An adult may experience feelings of fear and being 'out of control' and will react emotionally and behaviourally accordingly.[10] EMDR targets the initial traumatic experience and the accompanying negative affect allowing transformation through a rapid learning process.[10-12]

Traumatic memories and desensitisation

Freud believed that we tend to repress memories associated with negative experiences. His theory is that the ego defends itself from anxiety by repression of potentially threatening memories.[13] The theory of repressed memories has been influential in the treatment of certain clinical conditions such as disorders arising from trauma and anxiety disorders.[14] In fact it is argued that when a distressing experience results in persistent anxiety, it has been stored without adequate processing or adaptive resolution. The event is 'frozen in time' in the moment of fear and pain and this lays the foundation for future inappropriate dysfunctional responses to similar events.[15]

When implicit memories (no longer in conscious awareness) have not been processed this may be at the root of a variety of psychological issues in the present;[16] physiological and mental processes are inextricably linked and fear becomes associated with certain stimuli causing a variety of anxiety disorders.[10] In other words the dysfunctional nature of traumatic memories, including the way in which they are stored, allows the negativity and beliefs from the past to control the individual in the present. Emotions, sensations and perspectives of earlier events colour the perceived view of similar present-day events and a current situation will automatically link into the memory network in which the earlier event is stored, eliciting both sounds and smells connected to the experience.[12]

Memories accompanying traumatic experiences are desensitised during EMDR and the accompanying thoughts, beliefs and feelings regarding the trauma are reprocessed. This comprehensive reprocessing enables changes in the anxiety and fear associated with the event. By concentrating treatment on the most dysfunctional memories EMDR targets the actual event, together with any flashbacks, nightmare images, and triggers that elicit the dysfunctional cognitions, emotions or sensations. There may be several disturbing memories and each one must be fully processed through the visual image of the experience, the negative and positive cognitions, the emotions, the level of disturbance and the physical sensations experienced in the body.[12] Once the negative memory has been identified together with the irrational belief regarding the associative memory, then the process of desensitisation can begin, generally starting with the most powerful memory (the worst time), then the earliest time and the most recent occurrence.[17]

Controlled research: memories

The treatment effects of EMDR on autobiographical memories have been researched scientifically.[18–21] The findings suggest that traumatic memories are processed at cognitive level following successful EMDR therapy. Using magnetic resonance imaging (MRI) scans during EMDR treatment, an increase in limbic processing (the limbic system is associated with emotions) was found, along with decreased frontal lobe activation (the system involved in attention and short-term memory).[22] Further investigations showed distinct effects of bilateral eye movements with regard to reduction of negative emotions, imagery vividness, memory retrieval and reductions in psycho-physiological symptoms.[23]

There is evidence to suggest that the protocols and procedures adopted in EMDR are effective in contributing to positive treatment effects and, by this process, dysfunctional behaviours and disparate memories are desensitised.[10]

Theory and protocols

EMDR adopts a model that emphasises cognitive information processing of past negative experiences and memories, the bilateral movements adopted inducing a light hypnotic trance. The procedures adopted in EMDR have been developed to identify, access and target dysfunctionally stored experiences. This allows for adaptive resolution of the information and shifts the information to the appropriate memory systems.[24,25]

The theory is that, through guided eye movements (or other sources of bilateral brain stimulation such as hand taps or alternating sounds), traumatic information held in neurological networks is changed and connected to more positive cognitions stored in subjective memory.[26] The protocols and treatment are used in conjunction with two different scales. The Subjective Unit of Disturbance (SUD) measure was first developed to treat patients in the field of behavioural psychology.[27] This uses a scale of 10 to 1 (or 10 to 0), where 10 represents the highest negative cognition when paired with the target image, and 1 (or 0) represents the lowest feelings of negativity. This enables the patient to rate the level of disturbance for a specific memory. Once desensitisation is completed (when the patient reports 1 or 0 on the SUD scale) the bilateral stimulation is continued while an alternative positive cognition is held. This installation phase is continued until a high level of belief in the new cognition is reported on the Validity of Cognition (VOC) measure, which uses a scale of 1 to 7, where 7 is the highest level of positive belief. The two scales used in conjunction with each other provide information concerning the immediate effects of treatment on a single memory.

An eight-phase psychotherapeutic treatment approach has been adopted with standardised procedures and protocols to address the full range of clinical conditions caused or exacerbated by previous negative experiences.[12] Subsequently this developed into the adaptive information processing (AIP) model, the premise of which is that every person has both an innate tendency to move towards health and wholeness and the inner capacity to achieve it.[15] The AIP model has been adopted for experiences for the highest level of trauma, 'A' category, as well as for small trauma designated as 't' trauma. The treatment of both 'A' and 't' trauma guides the procedures and protocols of the clinical practice of EMDR,[12] and the methodology used has been extensively validated.[4,28–32]

Clinical studies: trauma

Evidence for the positive effects of EMDR in the treatment of trauma has been provided in numerous studies showing positive pre- to post-changes in symptom relief post-therapy.[33,34] It has been used successfully in a number of different situations and across various domains including: comorbid conditions resulting from global trauma such as earthquake, terrorist attacks and victims of war;[35,36] substantial reductions in psycho-physiological symptoms in patients suffering from PTSD;[4,28,32] depression; and social functioning.[7]

A complete model of how EMDR could lead to specific improvements in PTSD and related anxiety conditions has been presented.[37] It suggests that alternating bilateral stimulation enhances communication between the left and right cognitive hemispheres of the brain and that during EMDR the flow of information from the hippocampus (which stores information) to the neo-cortex (which analyses information) is directionally reversed. This allows for cognitive re-evaluation of previously maladjusted/negative encoded information similar to rapid eye movements (REM) in sleep cycles. Indeed evidence has been given that the process of EMDR rapidly desensitises the sufferer's anxiety through bilateral stimulation.[38]

While cognitive-based therapies and interventions such as relaxation techniques, meditation or positive imagery have typically been used to treat performance anxiety,[39] emerging understanding of the cognitive/emotional interface regarding anxiety and stress per se has led to innovative evidence-based techniques being employed for the reduction of anxiety.[40,41]

EMDR treatment for performance anxiety

The research literature indicates that there is a high incidence of performance anxiety in the domains of sport, music/the arts and public speaking. EMDR protocols are now being applied to alleviate anxiety and enhance performance in these fields.[42] However, there is a paucity of scientific research using EMDR as an intervention in these areas in comparison with therapies that are in vogue.

In the sports domain little research has been conducted into anxiety experienced in dressage[43] or swimming;[44] however more investigations have been conducted in the field of athletics. A study looking at the effect of EMDR on sports performance in athletes was conducted using three groups (control, EMDR and placebo). The groups were tested on five dependent variables pre- to post-treatment. Overall results revealed that the EMDR group reported more favourable gains than the control and the placebo groups, and significant results were found on the SUD and VOC scales.[45] This research was subsequently extended to encompass the role that saccadic and tracking gaze behaviour, used in EMDR therapy, exerted on an elite athlete population. However, it was shown that the sports performance results were inconclusive with no significant difference between the control and EMDR groups.[46] Using EMDR as an intervention for athletic performance enhancement it was found that both qualitative and quantitative results demonstrated that EMDR had a positive impact on measurable performance outcomes, performance anxiety, self-esteem and motivation. In addition a peak performance protocol has been developed using EMDR to enhance performance, enabling individuals to overcome subjective negativity.[47]

Music performance is another area with a high incidence of anxiety. Research was conducted investigating performance anxiety in singers which highlighted the idiosyncrasies within the vocal range, such as the vocal break between head and chest voice, and showed that EMDR was helpful in coping with this and general enhancement of performance.[48] This research was extended when the effects of EMDR were explored with a group of brass players suffering from maladaptive memories of past performances. It was found that EMDR was effective in aiding performance through desensitising and reprocessing dysfunctional memories.[49] Research into the influence of trauma on aspects of musicians' music making, particularly its effects on emotional expression and memory, showed that dissociative symptoms affected memory and concentration. EMDR was one of a number of psychotherapies investigated, including hypnotherapy and CBT; it was found that all were beneficial, and students and teachers were encouraged to adopt therapies to avoid risk of further traumatisation.[50] Building on this research a clinical outcome study was conducted with advanced pianists suffering from MPA investigating the effect of EMDR and CH for the alleviation of this condition (see Chapter 2, pp. 16–17).[51] During the research period both therapies significantly reduced MPA (state anxiety) post-therapy, however in addition, longitudinal monitoring of trait levels of anxiety at four months and one year post-therapy showed significant decreases in trait levels of anxiety below baseline levels in both groups.[52] This is an important finding (which has not been reported previously) as significant decreases in trait anxiety (a person's general anxiety level) equates to a change in the basic personality and has broader implications in other fields.

EMDR research was conducted into performance anxiety in acting.[53] The investigator reported on his own experiences of EMDR and the effect of therapy on his subjective anxiety when acting. He concluded that the methodology yielded favourable results. However the research is flawed as he was the sole investigator giving an autobiographical account of his experiences. The research would be difficult to verify as there appears to be no substantial data to support his claims. Anxiety generated by auditions in the arts was investigated using EMDR as a treatment.[54] It was found that it was particularly helpful in reducing performance anxiety and enhancing memory-based scripts for optimal performance.

The above studies give a brief overview of the application of EMDR documenting the effects of this innovative therapy in a number of different fields. As a therapeutic treatment for anxiety-based conditions, it addresses the underlying root cause of the problem as well as the presenting symptoms and offers positive healing and alleviation of the symptoms rapidly in comparison with other trauma therapies.

Summary

This chapter discussed the background, theory and expansion of EMDR explaining the procedures and protocols through use of the AIP model. It reviewed the important role that dysfunctional memories exert on present-day experiences and the influence that repressed memories can have on a variety of clinical conditions, such as disorders arising from trauma and anxiety. This chapter also looked at scientific evidence of treatment effects on autobiographical memories and how these are processed. A brief overview was given of the effects of EMDR treatment for a number of diverse conditions before looking at these effects specifically in the domains of music, sport and acting. There are many questions still to be answered concerning EMDR; as a relatively new psychotherapy it needs continuous rigorous investigation, both empirically and in laboratory studies, so that credence can be given to what appears to be an effective and innovative therapy.

Chapter 4 outlines the method adopted for the reflective case studies documented in Chapters 5–13 using EMDR and CH as therapeutic interventions for the reduction of performance anxiety.

References

1 Shapiro, F. (1991). Stray thoughts. *EMDR Network Newsletter*, *1*, 1–3.
2 Shapiro, F. (1994). Alternative stimuli in the use of EMDR. *Journal of Behavior Therapy and Experimental Psychiatry*, *25*, 89.
3 Shapiro, F. (2002). Paradigms, processing, and personality development. In F. Shapiro (ed.), *EMDR as an integrative psychotherapy approach: Experts of diverse orientations explore the paradigm prism* (pp. 3–26). Washington, DC: American Psychological Association.
4 Hogberg, G., Pagani, M., Sundin, O., Soares, J., Aberg-Wistedt, A., Tarnell, B., et al. (2007). On treatment with eye movement desensitization and reprocessing of chronic post-traumatic stress disorder in public transportation workers: A randomized controlled study. *Nordic Journal of Psychiatry*, *61*(1), 54–61.
5 Hogberg, G., Pagani, M., Sundin, O., Soares, J., Aberg-Wistedt, A., Tarnell, B., et al. (2008). Treatment of post-traumatic stress disorder with eye movement desensitization and reprocessing: Outcome is stable in 35-month follow-up. *Psychiatry Research*, *159*(1), 101–108.
6 Kemp, M., Drummond, P., & McDermott, B. (2010). A wait-list controlled study of eye movement desensitization and reprocessing (EMDR) for children with post-traumatic stress disorder (PTSD) symptoms from motor vehicle accidents. *Clinical Child Psychology and Psychiatry*, *15*, 5–25.
7 Power, K.G., McGoldrick, T., Brown, K., Buchanan, R., Sharp, D., Swanson, V., et al. (2002). A controlled comparison of eye movement desensitization and reprocessing versus exposure plus cognitive restructuring, versus waiting list in the treatment of post-traumatic stress disorder. *Journal of Clinical Psychology and Psychotherapy*, *9*, 299–318.
8 Schneider, J., Hofmann, A., Rost, C., & Shapiro, F. (2008). EMDR in the treatment of chronic phantom limb pain. *Pain Medicine*, *9*(1), 76–82.
9 Shapiro, F. (2007). EMDR and case conceptualization from an adaptive information processing perspective. In F. Shapiro, F.W. Kaslow, & L. Maxfield (eds),

Handbook of EMDR and family therapy processes (pp. 3–34). Hoboken, NJ: John Wiley & Sons.

10 Aigen, K. (1996). The role of values in qualitative music therapy research. In M. Langenberg, K. Aigen & J. Frommer (eds), *Qualitative research in music therapy: Beginning dialogues* (pp. 9–33). Gilsun, NH: Barcelona Publishers.

11 Shapiro, F., & Forrest, M.S. (1997). *EMDR: The breakthrough 'eye movement' therapy for overcoming anxiety, stress and trauma.* New York: Basic Books.

12 Shapiro, F. (1995). *Eye movement desensitization and reprocessing: Basic principles, protocols and procedures.* New York: Guilford Press.

13 Freud, S. (1962). The ego and the id. In J. Strachey (ed.), *The standard edition of the complete psychological works of Sigmund Freud,* vol. *XIX* (pp. 3–62). New York: W.W. Norton.

14 Baddeley, A.D., Eysenck, M.W., & Anderson, M.C. (2009). *Memory.* Hove: Psychology Press.

15 Shapiro, F. (2001). *Eye movement desensitization and reprocessing: Basic principles, protocols and procedures* (2nd edn.). New York: Guilford Press.

16 Baddeley, A.D. (1999). *Essentials of human memory.* Hove: Psychology Press.

17 Luber, M. (2009). *Eye movement desensitization and reprocessing (EMDR) scripted protocols: Basics and special situations.* New York: Springer.

18 Andrade, J., Kavanagh, D., & Baddeley, A. (1997). Eye-movements and visual imagery: A working memory approach to the treatment of post-traumatic stress disorder. *British Journal of Clinical Psychology, 36,* 209–223.

19 Barrowcliff, A.L., Gray, N.S., Freeman,T.C.A., & MacCulloch, M.J. (2004). Eye movements reduce the vividness, emotional valence and electrodermal A associated with negative autobiographical memories. *Journal of Forensic Psychiatry and Psychology, 15,* 325–345.

20 Christman, S.D., Garvey, K.J., Propper, R.E., & Phaneuf, K.A. (2003). Bilateral eye movements enhance the retrieval of episodic memories. *Neuropsychology, 17,* 221–229.

21 Pagani, M., Di Lorenzo, G., Verardo, A.R., Nicolais, G., Monaco, L., Lauretti, G., et al. (2012). Neurobiological correlates of EMDR monitoring – An EEG study. *PLoS ONE, 7*(9), e45753.

22 Herkt, D., Tumani, V., Grön, G., Kammer, T., Hofmann, A., & Abler, B. (2014). Facilitating access to emotions: Neural signature of EMDR stimulation. *PLoS ONE, 9*(8), e106350.

23 Coubard, O.A. (2015). Eye movement desensitization and reprocessing (EMDR) re-examined as cognitive and emotional neuroentrainment. *Frontiers in Human Neuroscience, 8,* 1035.

24 Siegel, D.J. (2002). The developing mind and the resolution of trauma: Some ideas about information processing and an interpersonal neurobiology of psychotherapy. In F. Shapiro (ed.), *EMDR as an integrative psychotherapy approach: Experts of diverse orientations explore the paradigm prism* (pp. 85–122). Washington, DC: American Psychological Association.

25 Stickgold, R. (2002). EMDR: A putative neurobiological mechanism of action. *Journal of Clinical Psychology, 58*(1), 61–75.

26 Grand, D. (2003). *Emotional healing at warp speed: The power of EMDR*. New York: Present Tents Publishing.

27 Wolpe, J. (1958). *Psychotherapy by reciprocal inhibition*. Stanford, CA: Stanford University Press.

28 Cvetek, R. (2008). EMDR treatment of distressful experiences that fail to meet the criteria for PTSD. *Journal of EMDR Practice and Research, 2*, 2–14.

29 De Jongh, A., van den Oord, H.J.M., & Ten Broeke, E. (2002). Efficacy of eye movement desensitization and reprocessing in the treatment of specific phobias: Four single-case studies on dental phobia. *Journal of Clinical Psychology, 58*(12), 1489–1503.

30 Jaberghaderi, N., Greenwald, R., Rubin, A., Zand, S.O., & Dolatabali, S. (2004). A comparison of CBT and EMDR for sexually abused Iranian girls. *Clinical Psychology and Psychotherapy, 11*, 358–368.

31 Ray, A.L., & Zbik, A. (2001). Cognitive behavioural therapies and beyond. In C.D. Tollison, J.R. Satterhwaite, & J.W. Tollison (eds), *Practical pain management* (3rd edn., pp. 189–208). Philadephia, PA: Lippincott.

32 Sack, M., Lempa, W., Steinmetz, A., Lamprecht, F., & Hofmann, A. (2008). Alterations in autonomic tone during trauma exposure using eye movement desensitization and reprocessing (EMDR): Results of a preliminary investigation. *Journal of Anxiety Disorders, 22*, 1264–1271.

33 Lamprecht, F., Kohnke, C., Lempa, W., Sack, M., Matzke, M., & Munte, T. (2004). Event-related potentials and EMDR treatment of posttraumatic stress disorder. *Neuroscience Research, 49*, 267–272.

34 Lansing, K., Amen, D.G., Hanks, C., & Rudy, L. (2005). High resolution brain SPECT imaging and EMDR in police officers with PTSD. *Journal of Neuropsychiatry and Clinical Neurosciences, 17*, 526–532.

35 Konuk, E., Knipe, J., Eke, I., Yusek, H., Yurtsever, A., & Ostep, S. (2006). Effects of EMDR therapy on post-traumatic stress disorder in survivors of the 1999 Marmara, Turkey earthquake. *International Journal of Stress Management, 13*, 291–308.

36 Silver, S.M., Rogers, S., Knipe, J., & Colelli, G. (2005). EMDR therapy following the 9/11 terrorist attacks: A community-based intervention project in New York City. *International Journal of Stress Management, 12*, 29–42.

37 Stickgold, R. (2002). EMDR: A putative neurobiological mechanism of action. *Journal of Clinical Psychology, 58*(1), 61–75.

38 Hays, K.F. (2009). Performance anxiety. In K.F. Hays (ed.), *Performance psychology in action* (pp. 101–120). Washington, DC: American Psychological Association.

39 Damasio, A.R. (1989). Time-locked multiregional retroactivation: A systems-level proposal for the neural substrates of recall and recognition. *Cognition, 33*, 25–62.

40 Scherer, K.R. (1993). Neuroscience projections to current debates in emotion psychology. *Cognition and Emotion, 7*, 1–41.

41 Wilson, D., Silver, S.M., Covi, W., & Foster, S. (1996). Eye movement desensitization and reprocessing: Effectiveness and autonomic correlates. *Journal of Behavior Therapy and Experimental Psychiatry, 27*, 219–229.

42 Foster, S., & Lendl, J. (1995). Eye movement desensitization and reprocessing: Initial applications for enhancing performance in athletes. *Journal of Applied Sport Psychology, 7*(suppl.), 63.

43 Crabbe, B. (1996). Can eye-movement improve your riding? *Dressage Today,* November, 28–33.

44 Graham, L. (2004). Traumatic swimming events reprocessing with EMDR. *The Sport Journal, 7*(1), 1–5.

45 Gracheck, K.A. (2011). Evaluating the efficacy of EMDR as an athletic performance enhancement intervention. Dissertation, University of the Rockies, Colorado.

46 Marshall. T.A. (2003). The role of gaze behaviour in eye movement desensitisation reprocessing (EMDR): Application to an elite athlete population. MA thesis, University of Calgary.

47 Lendl, J., & Foster, S. (2009). EMDR performance enhancement psychology protocol. In M. Luber (ed.), *EMDR scripted protocols: Basics and special situations* (pp. 377–396). New York: Springer Publishing.

48 Feener, R.S. (2005). EMDR: Eye movement desensitization and reprocessing: A new method in the treatment of performance anxiety for singers. DM thesis, Florida State University.

49 Plummer, C.D. (2007). Performance enhancement for brass musicians using eye movement desensitization and reprocessing. DM thesis, University of Cincinatti.

50 Swart, I. (2009). The influence of trauma on musicians. DMus thesis, University of Pretoria.

51 Brooker, E. (2018). Music performance anxiety: A clinical outcome study into the effects of cognitive hypnotherapy and eye movement desensitisation and reprocessing in advanced pianists. *Psychology of Music, 46*(1), 107–124.

52 Brooker, E. (2015). Music performance anxiety: An investigation into the efficacy of cognitive hypnotherapy and eye movement desensitisation and reprocessing when applied to Grade 8 pianists. Doctoral dissertation eThesis, University of Leeds. Retrieved from http://etheses.whiterose.ac.uk/12130.

53 Oglesby, C.A. (1999). An investigation into the effect of eye movement desensitization and reprocessing on states of consciousness, anxiety, self-perception, and coach- perceived performance ratings of selected varsity collegiate athletes. Dissertation, Temple University, Pennsylvania.

54 Grand, D. J. (2009). Audition anxiety. In K. F. Hays (ed.), *Performance psychology in action* (pp. 121–138). Washington, DC: American Psychological Association.

Part II
Nine case studies

4 Reflective case studies
Method and procedure

As a research method the case study is used in many situations to increase our knowledge of an individual or group in specific circumstances, and allows investigators to view the holistic and meaningful characteristics of real-life events. It is an empirical enquiry that looks at a contemporary phenomenon in depth and within its real-life context; it enables the tracing of events over time and unearths key subjective phenomena.[1] In fact it is argued that the essence of a case study is that it aims to illuminate a decision or set of decisions: why they were taken, how they were implemented, and with what result.[2]

The case studies in the following chapters focus on an idiographic approach (a study of the individual) as this gives much greater insight into subjective cognitions and emotions in a performance situation than would be possible from a nomothetic approach (a study of groups). This section of the book gives a broad overview of the assessment and treatment of anxiety-based conditions. The author, who is also the therapist, gives individual case conceptualisation of the nine studies, describing in detail the effect of the interaction of the therapy with the individual's experience. Each case study reports on the effects of the given therapy on the subject's anxiety, and compares the possible use of alternative therapies and the plausibility of their effectiveness. The studies also emphasise the relationship between the therapist's assessment of the presenting issues and the clinical intervention adopted and give the researcher's reflections on the suitability of the treatment provided.

The cases were selected as each had a particularly interesting outcome post-therapy which the author deemed useful for scientific research. A mix of non-randomised therapies (seven from private practice) and randomised (two from PhD research) are included, allowing the reader to make comparisons. In the first therapy session each individual's account/history of their experiences in performance, as well as in other areas, is documented as their narrative/story. Interpretation of the narrative by the therapist is an attempt to understand human behaviour with all its many complexities, and the idiographic approach has a very important role to play in achieving this. Indeed it is argued that a coherent self-narrative is a precondition for psychological well-being.[3]

The main aim of the case studies was to investigate further the effects of CH and EMDR, the interventions adopted for treatment of performance anxiety, and to provide opportunities to analyse and critique the therapies adopting a qualitative approach; however in two studies both qualitative and quantitative assessments were made as part of the PhD research. In eight cases the outcomes of the interventions are reported longitudinally providing valuable insight into the long-term effectiveness of the therapies.

Method

The book focuses on nine individuals suffering from performance anxiety in one of three different domains: music, sport or the workplace. The music sample comprised one male and four females, their instruments being piano, clarinet and voice. The sport sample consisted of two female horsewomen (one professional and one semi-professional). Two individuals (one male one female) experienced anxiety in the workplace at presentations, meetings and conferences. All signed consent forms to their cases being included in the book. The names have been changed to ensure anonymity.

Overall design and structure

Each study contains an abbreviated description of the progression of treatment, giving insight into the process of therapy by exploring the internal thoughts, feelings and experiences of the participants. The case studies are presented using the participant's own words as the subjective voice is important. 'Subjective' refers to the participant's own interpretation of events and feelings and 'objective' to the therapist's interpretation of these.

Tools

In order to test anxiety in what was deemed to be a threatening situation the State-Trait Anxiety Inventory (STAI)[4] was completed 15 minutes prior to a public performance in three cases reported here. This widely used questionnaire uses a four-point Likert-type scale, and assesses both state (STAI Y-1) and trait (STAI Y-2) anxiety levels, each having a range of scores between 20 (low anxiety) and 80 (high anxiety). Both parts of the questionnaire were completed initially in a non-threatening situation to establish baseline levels of anxiety and again immediately prior to a performance situation to identify changes in state anxiety according to environmental pressure.[4]

In the first two cases presented here a self-report questionnaire (designed by the author) was completed at two different points in time, immediately after playing in two performances, the first pre-therapy and the second post-therapy. This was designed to give qualitative information on the real-life experience of performance anxiety. It assessed cognitive anxiety and behaviour pre- and during performance, as well as physiological symptoms of somatic anxiety (somatic anxiety is the physical manifestation of anxiety in the body such as trembling, sweating etc.) An example of this completed questionnaire can be found in Appendices 5.1 and 5.2 in Chapter 5.

In order to enhance the effect of therapy, a CD (designed by the therapist) was given to each subject: *Relaxation, Self-Confidence for Musicians* or *Self-Confidence*. Depending on the nature and severity of the condition the choice of CD was made at the discretion of the clinician.

Usually after an EMDR therapy the *Relaxation* CD would be given to aid any residual stress which can occur before completion of treatment.

Procedure

The therapy was constructed so that in the initial interview the subjective narrative was related to the therapist. Subjective remembering of experiences which are retold in therapy is a process of 'narrativisation' termed 'narrative smoothing' and allows the traumatic experience to be revisited in a safe environment and expressed verbally.[5] It is thought that it gives greater understanding of the emotional experience and that by reconstructing the narrative, the individual asserts more control over the story leading to psychological well-being. It is believed that by taking the narrative approach, causative factors can be determined that underlie and maintain the root cause of the problem.[3] Each case study presented here begins with the subjective narrative.

The general protocols and procedures adopted by the clinical practitioner prior to the onset of treatment are outlined in Table 4.1. They are a broad adaptation of evidence-based formulation-driven treatment.[6]

The therapeutic session generally moves through three distinct stages:

1   Discrete observation, subjective history and narrative smoothing: from the commencement of the first session the therapist observes any discomfort displayed by the subject (usually physiological/somatic). This can be during the subjective history or during narrative smoothing (relating the details of past/present experiences).

2   Intervention: an explanation of the intervention to be applied given by the therapist. Questions or misapprehensions that the subject might have regarding the therapy is addressed at this point before the therapy is applied.

3   Changed behaviour post-intervention: during or after the treatment/ treatments, the subject discusses with the therapist any noticeable changes in behaviour.

Table 4.1 Case conceptualisation and therapeutic change methods

1	Referral
2	Case history
3	Circumstances: past context to present (then and now)
4	Presenting problem
5	Motivation and incentives for change
6	Prime issues to address: negative cognitions, physiological/somatic symptoms, behavioural
7	Critical analysis by therapist: aims/objectives
8	Treatment plan
9	Subjective/objective assessment of treatment
10	Researcher's reflections on treatment suitability
11	Longitudinal outcome

Summary

In this chapter the value of the case study has been reviewed as a research tool, focusing on the importance of an idiographic approach which adopts subjective narrativisation. Like other research methods it is a means of investigating an empirical phenomenon by following a set of procedures. Case study research has traditionally been considered to be a 'soft' option, possibly because investigations have not followed systematic procedures. We looked at the method by which the studies in this book were conducted, allowing for the in-depth documentation of the individual's experience of performance anxiety. A review of CH and EMDR for the treatment of multifarious conditions was given in Part I; Part II now documents nine case studies following systematic procedures investigating the problem of performance anxiety and the effects of CH and EMDR for the alleviation and eradication of this condition.

References

1 Yin, R.K. (2009). *Case study research: Design and methods*. Thousand Oaks, CA: Sage Publications.
2 Schramm, W. (1971). *Notes on case studies of instructional media projects*. Working paper. Washington, DC: Academy for Educational Development.

3 Spence, D. (1982). *Narrative truth and historical truth: Meaning and interpretation in psychoanalysis*. New York: W.W. Norton.

4 Spielberger, C.D., Gorsuch, R.L., & Lushene, R.E. (1977). *State–trait anxiety inventory for adults*. Palo Alto, CA: Consulting Psychologists Press.

5 Schafer, R. (1978). *Language and insight*. New Haven, CT: Yale University Press.

6 Persons, J. B. (1989). *Cognitive therapy in practice: A case formulation approach*. New York: W.W. Norton.

5   ADHD, perfectionism and fear of failure

A link to music performance anxiety?

Identifying information

Name:	Jane
Extreme anxiety:	Piano
Gender:	Female
Age:	21 years
Occupation:	Third year undergraduate student at the University of Leeds; a participant in the author's research into music performance anxiety; advanced level of piano

Case history: Jane's narrative from the first treatment session

Since my mid-teens I suffered from anxiety and hyperactivity and was diagnosed with Attention Deficit Hyperactivity Disorder (ADHD). I feel depressed almost continually. During year 3 at junior school I was bullied and this continued for a whole year. I felt different to everyone else as I had so much energy and didn't know where it was coming from. I didn't understand this, it made me feel both sad and angry and that things were not fair. Academically I was very good at school, although I always had to work very hard. Before I reached my teenage years around the age of 8/9 I had a fear of failure and felt that perfectionism had crept in which plagued me right throughout my teenage years. When I first came to university friends seemed to sympathise with me, but I soon felt isolated and that no-one understood my condition. I have continual negative thoughts, and feelings of 'black' depression. I've had CBT and counselling and neither have worked.

My past experiences of music performance have varied. I felt that I never had enough time to practise as much as I would have liked, and that it was always 'slap dash' with my piano and clarinet practice. I never enjoyed performing and became very nervous and worried weeks before the performance. The most recent experience in music performance was Grade 8 piano where I was crying and shaking during the examination with my hands slipping off the keys. It was similar for my Grade 8 clarinet where I felt very confused. What makes matters worse is the fact that my younger sister loves performing.

My performance this afternoon was an awful experience [see self-report questionnaire, Appendix 5.1]. I had worried weeks before that I wouldn't be prepared enough and that everyone else would have a perfect performance. My feelings grew stronger as the weeks went by and at one time I had wanted to pull out but I was persuaded not to. My hands were already shaking and sweaty fifteen minutes before playing and during the performance it got much worse. My heart was beating quickly and I was trembling throughout my whole body, my vision was really cloudy and I was unable to hit the keys, it seemed as if I was having a panic attack.

Case formulation

Therapist's interpretation

Caution must be taken in developing a case formulation from one in-depth interview. What follows is the therapist's interpretation of the possible dynamics underlying the anxiety/depression and distress and severe intractable symptoms of this participant.

Jane presented with the following negative schemas (these are her direct quotes):

'not good enough no matter what I do'

'hurting myself'

'I am afraid'

'I feel isolated and lonely'

'I am scared'

Jane's physiological/somatic sensations prior to and during performance were:

quickened heart rate;

violent shaking of whole body; and

tension throughout body/tight muscles.

Therapist's summary of Jane's comments

There are strong incentives for change in this participant. Jane's depressed
state (which has never been clinically diagnosed) and ADHD, which
has, are affecting her life in a negative way. It is reported that these two
conditions can be intertwined with some symptoms of ADHD overlap-
ping with signs of depression, making it difficult to differentiate between
them. Restlessness, worry and fear of failure can be symptomatic of both
states.[1] Her feelings of isolation and abandonment are compounded by loss
of friends, who although initially sympathetic now show impatience and
lack of understanding, adding to her depression. Important forthcoming
assessments at university are impacting on the anxiety and compounding
the situation. Her self-perception is extremely negative, with low feelings
of self-esteem. There is a strong negative bias regarding social activities
and circles of friends, as well as in her academic work. She is particularly
fearful of situations where she feels that she is in the spotlight, in particular
solo performance of any kind. Jane wants to feel in control and be able to
perform in any situation, without the crippling negativity which has haunted
her for years.

Critical analysis: therapist

There is sufficient evidence here to conclude that Jane is suffering from
social anxiety/social phobia: she anticipates disaster, failure and negative
scrutiny by others, and this is her prime focus. Social phobia is a response
to threats to social status and reputation, a fear of not matching up to one's
own expectations.[2] This is clearly indicated by her narrative comments:
'around the age of 8/9 I had a fear of failure and felt that perfectionism
had crept in which plagued me right throughout my teenage years'. Her
depressed state is due to the combination of her perfectionism together with
her cognitive negativity.

Aims and objectives

The critical objective is to change the subjective negativity held since the
age of 8 years into positive perceptions. This will increase feelings of self-
esteem and affect positively this participant's depressive state. Self-focused
negative attention of forthcoming events plays a key role in the maintenance of anxiety in performance.[3] Physiological reactions to emotional
experiences, and the cognitive perception of these, are stored in memory
together.[4] Desensitising the memory of both past and present traumatic
experiences and then reprocessing these into more positive perceptions

should achieve the therapist's primary objective. The extreme anxiety and somatic symptoms experienced during this participant's music performance should decrease once the negative perceptions have been changed, making the behavioural aspect of performance far more pleasurable.

Treatment plan: EMDR

As a participant in the author's empirical research at the University of Leeds, Jane had been randomly allocated to the EMDR therapy group within the three groups (CH, EMDR and Control).

Before the onset of treatment the process of EMDR is explained carefully. The technique employs bilateral movements; this helps to eliminate emotional distress associated with trauma (Chapter 3, pp. 24–25). It works on the principle of targeting the most traumatic memory first. Participants are informed that recall of traumatic memories may cause upsetting physical symptoms as well as disturbing thoughts and images, but that these should dissipate as the treatment progresses; they are given short frequent breaks during the procedure. During this time subjective thoughts, feelings and images are related to the therapist and are regularly monitored on the Subjective Unit of Disturbance (SUD) scale.

First treatment: 11 February 2013

This treatment (1 hour 15 minutes) was given as soon as possible after the first performance (within one hour).

Jane appeared nervous and on edge at the beginning of therapy but had somewhat recovered from her earlier symptoms. A full history was taken of past experiences (subjective narrative smoothing) during which time she became very upset. It is reported that narratives tap implicit psychological processes not accessible via self-report.[5] The main principles of EMDR were explained; however she was very sceptical: 'I've had CBT and counselling and neither worked.'

After Jane's narration she rated the experience causing the highest trauma on a Likert-type scale of 0 to 10, where 10 is the highest trauma (see Chapter 3, p. 25). The primary target was her 'black depression', subjectively described as the worst experience of her life, which she rated as 10 (high trauma) on the SUD scale. She became intensely agitated when recalling the worst part of the memory, and experienced extreme somatic symptoms: her whole body was shaking and her feet repeatedly banging the floor. However she wished to continue and required few breaks in the proceedings. After further desensitisation of the memory by the therapist to 5 on the SUD scale her somatic symptoms decreased markedly in the upper body; however they continued in the legs and feet. Further desensitisation resulted in a rating of 2 on the SUD. At this point she felt 'much calmer', all physical symptoms had dissipated and her feelings of loneliness had diminished. Further desensitisation brought the SUD to 1; the tension in her body had gone, and she was able to look more objectively and rationally at the worry and frustration that she had been feeling. The whole process of desensitisation of the strongest memory had taken 25 minutes yet it had had a significant impact.

In the same session the second target (bullying at school) was rated by Jane as 7/8 on the SUD scale. Recalling the memory of this experience, her strongest thoughts were of being different and not understanding why she had been singled out as a victim of bullying. Her strongest emotions when recalling this memory were of anger, frustration and sadness. Her original rating on the scale was lowered rapidly to 0. It is believed that this rating indicates a resolution of former dysfunctional cognitions and emotions.[6] On reviewing the memory Jane's perception had changed: 'It wasn't my fault, it doesn't seem important now, I don't need this any longer'.

At the end of the first treatment she described her feelings:

> I felt I'd been underneath a table for all of these years and now I'm above the table looking down upon it. I feel positive again, light and free, I haven't felt like this since before GCSEs, it feels like a detox.

Jane was given the author's *Relaxation* CD and asked to listen to this each day until the next therapy.

Second treatment: 18 February 2013

Jane had maintained the positive cognitive changes since the previous treatment as well as the emotional change of happiness and a feeling of 'lightness'. She felt calm, had feelings of positivity and no longer felt depressed. Jane had rung her parents on the evening of the first session and told them how different she felt and was told that they could hear the difference in her voice.

The second session targeted the traumatic performance experiences: Grade 8 piano and clarinet examinations, oral language examination at university, and the most recent experience: participating in performance 1 of the author's research into MPA.

Recalling these experiences revealed disappointment as the overriding emotional feeling; other emotions were anger and frustration. Negative cognitions were of worry and fear. Music examinations were rated as 7/8 on the SUD. Jane's subjective rating of negative thoughts and feelings of the experiences decreased to 1 on the SUD scale after 20–30 minutes. Having dissipated the negativity, the positivity was then reinforced through the Validity of Cognition (VOC) scale (see Chapter 3, p. 25). Jane chose three words of prime importance for her in enhancing future performances: *confident; calm; focused.* These became her key words. Using positive imagery regarding her performance together with the key words, her level on the VOC scale quickly rose to 7 (the highest level) indicating substantial positivity.

After a brief discussion, Jane indicated that she was feeling calm, positive and looking forward to the second performance in which she was playing Liszt's 'Au Lac de Wallenstadt' (the piece she had played ten days previously in the first performance).

Participant's assessment of treatment (subjective)

Pre-treatment: Jane's description

I don't think EMDR will be very effective, because I don't understand why I get so nervous. When I perform it's like my body takes over, and I have no control; it's just like irrational panic. Consequently, because I can't isolate an event or reason as to why I have such a reaction when performing, I never believed it had a solution. I've tried CBT and counselling before and neither worked.

(Oral quotation, 11 February 2013)

Post-treatment: Jane's testimonial

I only recently became aware that I had depression, but I had been unknowingly suffering from it for many years; that's one of the problems with depression, it can be a slow poison. It slowly corrupts and warps your notion of normality until you forget a happy version of yourself ever existed. I could never understand why I suffered from it, as I couldn't pinpoint an event or attribute a reason as to why I felt like I did. I always thought such therapies would only work if you knew why you were depressed, but I couldn't have been more wrong. Eye movement desensitisation and reprocessing (EMDR) helped me let go of my negative thoughts and snapped me out of depression's vicious cycle. After just one session, I left feeling so unburdened, I felt physically lighter; I remembered that forgotten feeling of happiness. For me, EMDR was like an EMotional Detox Remedy; once again I have the strength to fight back when life throws its curve balls.

(Email, April 2013)

Therapist's assessment of treatment (objective)

A clear underlying model structure of the treatment was offered to the patient. To maximise the effects, the therapy focused on both past and current problems relevant to this participant. Distant memories were targeted alongside more recent events and situations. It is argued that memories of present-day unique experiences are coded as inputs in the brain and filtered according to past experiences.[7]

By working through the experiences relating to the highest trauma level and desensitising the memories, the subjective negative schemas were addressed and replaced with a sense of positivity. The bodily sensations that had been experienced when recalling each trauma had gone. This participant no longer felt depressed; the cognitive negative bias was replaced with a positive bias. She had been randomly assigned to EMDR therapy and therefore it is possible that this may not have been the most effective therapy for her. However the clinician's assessment of the efficacy of the treatment was that it had been beneficial in this instance; the desired effect was achieved, bringing about rapid change. As well as a qualitative assessment of anxiety, a quantitative analysis of cognitive anxiety was obtained.[8] This allowed for comparisons with baseline levels of state–trait anxiety with levels fifteen minutes prior to performance 1 and 2 (pre- and post-therapy). Jane's baseline state (performance anxiety) indicated a score of 33 within the low category of STAI Y-1; however this rose sharply to 59 (one point below high category) 15 minutes prior to the first performance. This is a substantial increase in state anxiety and gives further evidence of social anxiety/phobia. Post-therapy this score decreased to 39 prior to performance 2 showing the effectiveness of the therapy for her music performance anxiety. Jane's trait baseline level of anxiety (general anxiety) pre-intervention was 50 (medium category) which decreased to 36 (low category) post-intervention, taken 15 minutes prior to the second performance (see Chapter 4, p. 36 for scoring of state and trait scales). This indicates that having desensitised the former traumatic experiences and memories the general level of anxiety also decreased substantially.

This study set out with the aim of assessing the effectiveness of EMDR for the treatment of MPA. In this instance the deep seated negative issues were the primary targets and were addressed first before focusing on the current problems relevant to this participant. A strong relationship was seen to exist between the past trauma and the present-day presenting issues (cognitive and physiological) which were resolved satisfactorily (the participant's comments verify this: see p. 45). The methods used were effective in achieving the desired goals, bringing about therapeutic change. This participant took part in the subsequent music performance, no longer experiencing the former anxiety or crippling physiological symptoms felt in the first performance.

However EMDR is a relatively new psychotherapy, and as such rigorous comparisons need to be made with other therapies and effects which could give a similar outcome to give credence and standing in the scientific world.

Researcher's reflections on treatment suitability

There can be no doubt that the treatment was effective; however reflecting on this as a researcher there are other possible explanations for the resolution of the problems presented here which need to be explored.

These outcomes may be explained by a number of different factors. For instance some individuals improve because they have entered therapy, regardless of the specific treatment: a variant of the placebo effect. Fascinating research has been conducted into the well-known phenomenon of the placebo effect with various medical conditions: headaches, pain reduction and even the visual effects of packaging in headache tablets. One study showed that the visual effects of packaging in headache tablets can exert a placebo effect.[9] A further study into this phenomenon found that headache pain was reduced where the treatment was placebo tablets.[10] Another study showed that pain reduction can occur when no specific pain relief has been given, only sugar-based placebo tablets.[11]

It could also be suggested that 'narrative smoothing' plays a large part in resolving psychological issues, and many psychotherapists support this view.[12–14] It is believed that the process of reconstruction of the initial narration gives more control over the story and can change the patient's perception into something more positive; this underpins the central goals of therapy.[15] Jane's narrative was highly charged with specific negative experiences and relating this allowed a different subjective perception.

Cognitive behavioural therapy (CBT) might also be effective as a therapy in this instance as it similarly uses narration in therapy but treats the presenting symptoms rather than the cause. CBT has similarities with psychodynamic therapies but there are a number of different elements which are distinctive (discussed in Chapter 2, p. 14). It treats the symptoms rather than the cause and as such this may only provide a short-term solution to the problem or, in this participant's case, no solution at all. Psychodynamic therapies specifically target internal conflicts, wishes and expectations.[16]

Jane's dysfunctional thoughts relate to her beliefs that she is 'not good enough no matter what I do' and 'I am afraid, I feel isolated and lonely, and scared'. On a deeper level these negative schemas are best addressed by focusing on the root cause of the problems, which is one of the main premises of EMDR. This participant has already received various forms of psychological treatments (CBT and counselling) which have failed to bring relief and have compounded her sense of anxiety in achieving a resolution to her symptoms.

The author is a neuro-linguistic programming (NLP) practitioner and it could be argued that NLP might also have positive effects for this partici- pant. NLP therapy focuses on positive imagery and reframing past negative images and experiences. The principles and techniques enable the individ- ual to deal with problematic situations in a creative and resourceful way. The main aim is the achievement of personal goals quickly and effectively. Although this participant would benefit from some of the protocols of NLP (positive reframing, achievement of personal goals), the experience of trauma, particularly if long-standing, needs to be targeted specifically. NLP works on the basis that by changing the upper conscious levels of neuro- logical thought this will always change the lower levels of consciousness.[7] However the author/clinician would argue that where there is long-standing trauma and social phobia, a more psychodynamic/psychoanalytical therapy is necessary, where the deep unconscious thoughts are the primary targets enabling treatment of the underlying root cause of the problem.

It can be argued that EMDR may be a variant on standard exposure treatments,[17] and that bilateral movement is not an essential part of the treatment.[18] However rigorous scientific testing has shown that bilateral movements assist the brain's information processing system, enabling rapid modification of problematically-stored memories.[19-21] It could be hypoth- esised that the rapid resolution of the issues presented by Jane in this case study corroborates the importance of bilateral movements in this therapy.

Longitudinal outcome

Within a few days of the therapy Jane played in the second performance of the author's Tranche 1 research. Her comments written on the self-report questionnaire, completed immediately after the first performance, are very revealing (Appendix 5.1). The self-report questionnaire completed after the second performance is also included in the appendix so that a comparison can be made (Appendix 5.2).

At a four month follow-up she still showed the beneficial effects achieved during the therapy. A quantitative assessment of the trait scores over time taken from the STAI Y-2 questionnaire showed a decrease of 9 points below baseline reading:

Baseline: 50

Performance 2 (post-therapy): 36

Four months post-therapy: 41

Her longitudinal experiences have been recorded in a log and are reported here. She has taken part in a solo performance/presentation (non-musical), which was an examination, and reported not feeling overly nervous beforehand:

> Before the therapy I would have imagined every worst possible outcome and then replay it in my head, I didn't do that, it was like I wasn't thinking about it at all; it was no longer something I feared, it was just another task, whatever happens, happens. I could almost detach myself from it. During my presentation I could feel my heart rate accelerate a little, but I managed to keep control, and steady my breathing. I just focused on my sheet in front of me.

Jane broke her arm in December 2013 which meant that she was unable to participate in sport and music activities. This resulted in chronic insomnia and the return of former levels of anxiety, as she was unable to manage the excess energy experienced from her hyperactivity disorder (ADHD). Her trait level of anxiety at this time returned to near baseline. However in an email dated 28 February 2014 she reported that the arm was fully recovered and that she was 'almost back to where I was before I broke my arm with respect to my moods and anxiety'. This incident was an unfortunate occurrence and makes it more difficult to assess the effect of EMDR one year post-therapy.

The second case study, Chapter 6, follows a similar overall format to the first but uses hypnotherapy as the intervention enabling comparisons between CH and EMDR.

Appendix 5.1 Self-report questionnaire pre-therapy treatment

1 What were your thoughts/feelings/emotions during the days/weeks leading up to the first performance?

   Nervous, was worried that I wouldn't be prepared enough and would make lots of mistakes. Kept thinking that everyone else would have a perfect performance and mine would stick out like a sore thumb.

2 Did your feelings stay the same/grow stronger/grow weaker as the concert approached?

   They got stronger but not by much - as already feeling nervous.

3 Did you ever feel so strongly that you felt you might withdraw?

   Yes I emailed Elizabeth alerting her that I didn't think I was ready, but she persuaded me to continue.

4 How did you feel 15/30 minutes before performing at the venue?

   Very nervous and tense, hands were already shaking and felt slightly sweaty.

(continued)

Appendix 5.1 (continued)

5   Did you experience any physical symptoms during your performance? What were they? To what degree?

Yes, my hands were shaking a little at first and my heart rate was high, then my head went cloudy and my hands were violently shaking and I couldn't hit the keys.

6   Did they improve or adversely affect your performance in any way?

Adversely affected, very much so; I completely fell apart - the shaking and blankness in my head seemed to dissolve my muscle memory in my fingers.

Appendix 5.2 Self-report questionnaire post-therapy treatment

---

1   What were your thoughts/feelings/emotions during the days/weeks leading up to the second performance?

Didn't think that much about it, was more intrigued to see if I was going to be calmer, definitely didn't feel nervous at this stage.

2   Did your feelings stay the same/grow stronger/grow weaker as the concert approached?

Yes, they felt the same.

3   Did you ever feel so strongly that you felt you might withdraw?

No.

4   How did you feel 15/30 minutes before performing at the venue?

Not tense, still didn't have many thoughts about playing - almost as if someone else was going to perform.

5   Did you experience any physical symptoms during your performance? What were they? To what degree?

My hands got a little sweaty, but I wasn't shaking before the performance. Part of the way through shook a bit but I had more control at stopping it - it didn't take over like last time. It happened 2/3 times.

6   Did they improve or adversely affect your performance in any way?

The performance was greatly improved this time. I was far more accurate and my head didn't go blank like before. I had more control, and was less tense. After I finished I was a little shaky in my hands but it soon went.

References

1   Diler, R.S., Daviss, W.B., Lopez, A., Axelson, D., Iyenqar, S., & Birmaher, B. (2007). Differentiating major depressive in youths with attention deficit hyperactivity disorder. *Journal of Affective Disorders, 102*(1–3), 125–130.

2 Nesse, R. (1998). Emotional disorders in evolutionary perspective. *British Journal of Medical Psychology, 71*, 397–415.

3 Coles, M.E., Hart, T.A., & Heimberg, R.G. (2005). Cognitive-behavioral group treatment for social phobia. In W.R. Crozier & L. E. Alden (eds), *Social anxiety for clinicians: The essential handbook* (pp. 265–286). Chichester: Wiley & Sons.

4 Lang, P.J. (1979). A bio-informational theory of emotional imagery. *Psychophysiology, 16*, 495–512.

5 Cousineau, T.M., & Shedler, J. (2006). Predicting physical health: Implicit mental health measures versus self-report scales. *The Journal of Nervous and Mental Disease, 194*(6), 427–432.

6 Hofmann, A., & Luber, M. (2009). In M. Luber (ed.), *Eye movement desensitization and reprocessing (EMDR) scripted protocols: Basics and special situations* (pp. 5–10). New York: Springer.

7 Alder, H., & Heather, B. (1999). *NLP in 21 days*. London: Piatkus.

8 Spielberger, C.D., Gorsuch, R.L., & Lushene, R.E. (1977). S*tate–trait anxiety inventory for adults*. Palo Alto, CA: Consulting Psychologists Press.

9 Blackwell, B., Bloomfield, S.S., & Buncher, C.R. (1972). Demonstration to medical students of placebo responses and non-drug factors. *Lancet, 1*(7763), 1279–1282.

10 Branthwaite, A., & Cooper, P. (1981). Analgesic effects of branding in treatment of headaches. *British Medical Journal (Clinical Research Edition), 282*, 1576–8.

11 Montgomery, G.H., & Kirsch, I. (1996). Mechanisms of placebo pain reduction: An empirical investigation. *Psychological Science, 7*, 174–176.

12 Brandchaft, B. (2007). Systems of pathological accommodation and change in analysis. *Psychoanalytic Psychology, 24*(4), 667–687.

13 Sroufe, L.A., & Waters, E. (1977). Attachment as an organizational construct. *Child Development, 48*, 1184–1199.

14 Stolorow, R.D. (2007). Anxiety, authenticity and trauma: The relevance of Heidegger's existential analytic for psychoanalysis. *Psychoanalytic Psychology, 24*(2), 373–383.

15 Schafer, R. (1978). *Language and insight*. New Haven, CT: Yale University Press.

16 Kenny, D.T. (2011). *The psychology of music performance anxiety*. Oxford: Oxford University Press.

17 McGlynn, F.D., & Lohr, J.M. (1998). Nonspecific factors in research on empirically supported treatments: Measurement and procedural controls. Paper presented at the Annual Convention of the Association for Advancement of Behavior Therapy, Washington, DC.

18 DeBell, C., & Jones, R.D. (1997). As good as it seems? A review of EMDR experimental research. *Professional Psychology: Research and Practice, 28*, 153–163.

19 Begley, S. (2009). *The plastic mind*. London: Constable.

20 Doidge, N. (2008). *The brain that changes itself: Stories of personal triumph from the frontiers of brain science*. London: Penguin Books.

21 LeDoux, J. (2002). *The synaptic self: How our brains become who we are*. New York: Viking.

6 Scepticism regarding treatment for piano performance

Why randomly selected therapy may not work

Identifying information

Name:	Dan
Music performance anxiety:	Piano (advanced)
Gender:	Male
Age:	20 years
Occupation:	Second year music student at the University of Leeds; a participant in the author's research into music performance anxiety

Case history: Dan's narrative from the first treatment session

My main instrument is piano but I also play electric guitar and keyboards as part of a group. I have generally never experienced much anxiety performing as part of a group, compared with solo piano performance. I may have at times felt slightly nervous, self-conscious or not fully relaxed playing guitar at gigs but not to a great degree, and I always enjoy it. It's a different story with piano, especially when I am being assessed for my performance. I do get angry with myself for making stupid mistakes and afterwards I never feel that I have practised enough. I always worry that things will go wrong and I will embarrass myself in front of everyone. My hands usually shake and can feel sweaty and can easily slip off the keys. I can get very stressed during a performance and annoyed with myself.

I can start to worry weeks before a piano performance, and this usually gets worse as the time gets closer, even if it's a class performance and everyone else is 'in the same boat'. It's so different playing my guitar or keyboard in the group, I don't feel isolated at all as I'm not playing on my own; we all support each other and are having fun. I don't remember always being like this with the piano until I took Grade 5 in my early teens. It wasn't a good experience, I got completely lost in one of the pieces and had to stop playing as I couldn't pick it up again. The examiner made me feel worse as he didn't seem at all sympathetic. Now I play from memory, even if I have the music in front of me, but I'm still worried that sometimes I'll have a memory lapse. With Grade 8 I just passed and I was hoping for a distinction. I would have done the Performance module here if I had had a distinction.

At the piano performance for your research a few days ago I was nervous, but not hugely so, as I knew that I wasn't being marked or judged, but 15/30 minutes before the performance started I felt strangely uneasy. I had the music on the stand for safety, even though I knew the piece from memory, but I was unable to concentrate on the music or where my fingers were and my hands felt slightly lighter; towards the end of the piece they were sweating. I had all these thoughts going through my mind about making silly mistakes and losing my place in the music and not being able to pick it up. I'd love to be able not to worry in the weeks before a solo performance and to feel confident when I'm playing and really focus on the music and enjoy it. I'd like to get rid of all the shakes and quivery feeling that I sometimes get and off-putting thoughts when I'm playing. I never have any of these physiological symptoms when playing the guitar or keyboard in the group and would love to be the same for piano.

Case formulation

Therapist's summary and interpretation of Dan's narrative

As a participant in the author's research into music performance anxiety (MPA) at the University of Leeds Dan had been randomly assigned cognitive hypnotherapy (CH).

His narration highlights his unique experiences in both piano as a soloist and as a group musician playing electric guitar and keyboard. The nature of the performance setting governs the level of his performance anxiety. His enjoyment of playing in the band where he only experiences slight nervousness contrasts with his anxiety and negative cognitions regarding solo piano performance where he displays fear of negative evaluation. His comment regarding the piano examination is very revealing: 'I don't remember always being like this with the piano until I took Grade 5 in my early teens. It wasn't a good experience.'

Critical analysis: therapist

This musician describes highly circumscribed experiences of MPA. His anxiety regarding solo piano performance is not a generalised fear of the performing situation, it is domain-specific. He is happy and only sometimes slightly nervous when playing as part of the band; however he can experience severe performance anxiety both before and during a piano performance.

The therapist's interpretation of his narrative is that Dan is suffering from focal anxiety, a condition that exists in an otherwise healthy, functioning musician. Focal anxiety is confined to very specific situations;[1] the disorder is the result of specific conditioning experiences.[2] The Grade 5 piano examination is such an example, a disorder that is a manifestation of an earlier experience. There may also be strong determinants to focal anxiety which exacerbate the situation, for example feeling underprepared for a performance can cause a strong anxiety response; his narrative describes how he feels that he has never practised enough.

Aims and objectives

The main objective is to change the negative perceptions that he has held regarding his solo piano performance since his early teens. The aims are to decrease his anxiety both in the weeks prior to and during the performance as well as to desensitise the physiological/somatic symptoms he experiences during performance which exacerbate the situation. A strong relationship has been shown to exist between mental cognitions, physiological symptoms and performance.[3]

The desired outcome is to make piano performance more enjoyable by alleviating the concern and anguish that he experiences. Realistic goals and positive cognitions need to be established. The somatic symptoms that he is experiencing, 'hands feeling lighter and sweaty', are highly likely to be manifestations of cognitive anxiety,[4] and would be expected to dissipate once cognitive perceptions have been changed.

Treatment plan: cognitive hypnotherapy

Dan had randomly been assigned to the CH group and would receive two one-hour treatments during the ten days between the first and second performances. The hypnotherapist induces a hypnotic state to increase motivation or alter the behaviour pattern of the participant by use of Ericksonian hypnotherapy (Chapter 2, p. 15). The treatment focuses on:

clinical history;

establishing rapport;

explanation of the therapeutic process; and

goal setting.

A detailed clinical history is taken to identify the psychological, physiological, social and environmental aspects of the experienced behaviours. Cognitive distortions, negative self-instructions, irrational thoughts and beliefs can then be targeted during hypnosis.

It is important to gain rapport with the participant. This can best be achieved by listening with empathy to the narrative description of the frustrations, distress and symptoms, and acknowledging their frustration and disappointments with the problem. The therapist then prepares the participant to enter the hypnotic state by explaining what will be experienced. It is argued that hypnotherapy allows for thoughts, feelings and association of situations to be viewed in more positive and improved ways.[5]

First treatment: 13 February 2013

The first treatment (one hour) was conducted two days after the first performance.

Dan had a negative bias regarding hypnosis. At the first session he intimated that he was very sceptical and believed that he would not be a receptive subject. He found it difficult to relax and thought that he would feel 'out of control'. However, his MPA regarding piano performance was so distressing that he wanted to participate and was intrigued with the explanation of the hypnotic procedure (explained in some depth). It was deemed by the therapist that rapport would be gained more quickly if the procedure was explained prior to discussing the self-report questionnaire and taking a full clinical history.

The conversation began by focusing on the self-report questionnaire, completed by Dan at the end of performance 1. In the days prior to the performance his anxiety had gradually increased and was particularly high the night before the performance. He was most nervous 15 minutes prior to and during the concert. This was substantiated by his state anxiety score on the STAI Y-1,[6] which had increased from 36 (baseline) to 42, indicating that he was experiencing enhanced cognitive anxiety. He had also experienced two off-putting somatic symptoms during the performance: lightness in the hands/fingers and sweaty hands.

Dan's narration of past musical experiences was followed by his aspirations for future performances and goal-setting (his subjective view of his optimal piano performances). He chose three key words to enhance performance: *control; focused; enjoyment.* Key words are anchored by the therapist by touch on the dominant wrist at appropriate times during therapy.

He was given the author's *Self-Confidence for Musicians* CD and asked to listen to this as often as possible until the next session, as it would enhance treatment.

Second treatment: 18 February 2013

The second treatment focused on reviewing his thoughts and feelings in the five days since the first therapy.

Dan reported that no beneficial effects had been noticed after the first treatment and he had been too busy to listen to the CD. He was however interested to see if there might be any differences in his second performance. He had completed the first question on the self-report questionnaire regarding the second performance; these comments were more positive than those regarding performance 1. He had written that he was not worried or nervous at all but felt a strong need to practise as assurance.

The remainder of the therapy followed the same format as the previous session with hypnotic induction and positive visualisation of performance situations, including the second performance. He was asked once more to listen to the author's CD and left looking forward to the second performance (although more from an experimental stance) as he still appeared to be sceptical.

Dan's self-assessment of treatment

Prior to treatment, all participants in the author's research had subjectively rated the effectiveness of the therapies on a Likert scale of 1 to 10, where 10 is the most effective and 1 is the least. Dan rated his initial perception of the therapies as 4, and post-therapy after the second performance as 6.

Dan completed the self-report questionnaire immediately after the second performance and wrote: 'I felt okay until approaching/entering the room, when I became a lot more nervous but focused, even more so than in the first performance. I wasn't having a great start to the day either which didn't help.' His written comments on his experience during his performance were:

> I felt uneasy and my limbs were quite quivery, more so than in the first performance. Interestingly I think this may have helped the overall sound (dynamics, crispness etc.) but I made three noticeable mistakes

in this performance rather than one mistake in the first performance. This could have been due to a more relaxed practice regime however, and behind the piano I didn't feel as comfortable as I did at the first performance from a technical perspective, but was more in control of the sound.

Therapist's assessment of treatment

In reviewing this case the therapist believes that overall CH was not effective for this participant for the reduction of MPA although it may have enhanced his playing somewhat at the second performance.

Dan entered a 'very light' trance state post-induction in both sessions; this is not as conducive to positive suggestion and goal setting as a deep hypnotic trance. After hypnotic induction eye catalepsy was introduced: the challenge to open the eyes. In a deep trance the participant is unable to do so, however Dan opened his eyes fully in the first session and partially in the second, indicating a light trance-state. This may be due to four factors:

a) During both treatments extraneous noises outside the room (which were sometimes sudden and loud) could be heard very clearly in the therapy room; extraneous noise if strong enough can inhibit full induction into a deep trance state.[5]
b) Feelings of not being 'in control' during the treatments. This would precipitate an inability to 'let go' and relax.[5]
c) Scepticism regarding the treatment. A strong relationship exists in non-belief of treatment effect with a neutral /negative outcome.[7]
d) Resistance to hypnosis. Even when full co-operation of the subject has been obtained, there can remain innate difficulty in some patients to respond to suggestions; this may interfere with the hypnotic process.[8]

Any one of these factors can inhibit entering into a deeper trance state.

His statements on the self-report questionnaire reveal that during the second performance (post-therapy) he felt more anxious than during the first performance. This is not borne out by his scores on the STAI Y-1 questionnaire completed 15 minutes prior to each performance as he scored 42 each time. However this does show that the therapy had not been effective in decreasing Dan's cognitive/state anxiety at the second performance. He made more notational errors in the second performance and felt less comfortable than in the first. However he does note that he felt more in control of the overall sound, dynamics and crispness of sound. This is interesting as Dan's primary key word for enhancement of performance was 'control'.

His perception of the second performance should also be noted; he states that he was more nervous, but more focused (a second key word). Although he made more mistakes in this performance he notices a positive difference in his playing. The therapist/researcher recorded both performances and can relate that his second performance (also assessed by an independent assessor) was a more thoughtful interpretation than the first, with more attention to dynamics and semiquaver runs more controlled.

The therapist is of the opinion that it would have been more beneficial for this participant if the traumatic experience of the piano examination in the early teenage years had been initially targeted through systematic desensitisation. However this was not in the remit of this therapy in the circumstance of this research. The therapist believes that EMDR would have been more effective in this instance.

As this participant is not a good subject for hypnotic induction, therapies conducted on a conscious level may be more beneficial for him.

Researcher's reflections on treatment suitability

There are several possible explanations for the non-effective outcome in the present case study.

This participant was highly sceptical of the hypnotic process; therapies that operate on a conscious as opposed to the unconscious level may be more effective. Mental skills training is such a therapy; used initially in the sports domain the main principles are now being applied to musical performance. It offers performers a range of musically validated techniques for honing their mental skills in order to enhance performance.[9] It concentrates on relaxation, cognitive imagery, performance goals, mental rehearsal, and role modelling, designed to reduce anxiety and enhance performance.

During the participant's first treatment a highly emotionalised fear was uncovered: the piano examination in his early teens. Re-educating implicit processes in the mind through creative reprogramming is the ultimate goal of hypnotherapy; however research shows that if trauma exists from a past experience, the trauma should be the primary target, using a desensitisation programme.[10] When the incident has been fully desensitised, through exposure therapy such as behavioural therapy (see Chapter 2, p. 13) or EMDR, and closure has been achieved, the participant will be ready for further therapy.[11] The unconscious mind can be re-educated through positive programming, and at this juncture CH could be introduced.

The outcome of this case study indicates that hypnotherapy is not effective for everyone and raises some important issues regarding randomised assignment of psychotherapies for research purposes. Randomised assignment may not always give a true effect of a therapy as the methodology must be adhered to and as such may give a less beneficial or even a negative outcome. In fact research has who found that randomised trials do not give a true indication of the real effect of the intervention.[12] Evidence suggests that matching of treatment to a patient's beliefs and characteristics increases the therapeutic outcome.[13] In contrast to the random assignment of therapies in the present research, in private practice once the clinical history has been taken and diagnosed the therapist ensures that the most appropriate treatment is given to obtain the most beneficial outcome.

Longitudinal outcome

In two follow-ups, at four months and one year post-therapy, Dan reported that as he is not on the Performance module at the university, there have been no solo piano performances and only two band performances (guitar). The therapist/researcher is therefore unable to reach a conclusion as to the effect of the therapy.

References

1 Kenny, D.T. (2011). *The psychology of music performance anxiety*. Oxford: Oxford University Press.

2 Stein, M.B., & Stein, D.J. (2008). Social anxiety disorder. *The Lancet*, *371*(9618), 1115–1125.

3 Barlow, D.H. (ed.). (2002a). *Anxiety and its disorders: The nature and treatment of anxiety and panic* (2nd edn). New York: Guilford Press.

4 Lang, P.J., Miller, G.A., & Levin, D. (1988). Anxiety and fear. In R.J. Davidson, G.E. Schwartz, & D. Shapiro (eds), *Consciousness and self-regulation* (pp. 123–151). New York: Plenum.

5 Alladin, A. (2008). *Cognitive hypnotherapy: An integrated approach to the treatment of emotional disorders*. Chichester: John Wiley & Sons.

6 Spielberger, C.D., Gorsuch, R.L., & Lushene, R.E. (1977). *State–trait anxiety inventory for adults*. Palo Alto, CA: Consulting Psychologists Press.

7 DePiano, F.A., & Salzberg, H.C. (1981). Hypnosis as an aid to recall and meaningful information presented under three types of arousal. *International Journal of Clinical and Experimental Hypnosis*, *29*, 283–400.

8 Barnett, E.A. (1989). *Analytical hypnotherapy: Principles and practice*. Glendale, CA: Westwood Publishing.

9 Connolly, C., & Williamon, A. (2004). Mental skills training. In A. Williamon (ed.), *Musical excellence: Strategies and techniques to enhance performance* (pp. 221–245). New York: Oxford University Press.

10 Skinner, B.F. (1953). *Science and human behaviour*. New York: Macmillan.

11 Shapiro, F., & Forrest, M.S. (1997). *EMDR: The breakthrough 'eye movement' therapy for overcoming anxiety, stress and trauma*. New York: Basic Books.
12 Yin, R.K. (2009). *Case study research: Design and methods*. Thousand Oaks, CA: Sage Publications.
13 Beutler, L.E., Clarkin, J.E., & Bongar, B. (2000). *Guidelines for the Systematic Treatment of the Depressed Patient*. New York: Oxford University Press.

7   An adult beginner's fears

The spectre of a piano examination

Identifying information

Name: Mary

Music performance anxiety: piano

Gender: Female

Age: 65

Occupation: Retired

Background information

Mary is an 'adult beginner' from the author's private practice who commenced piano lessons in 2007. As a child and teenager she was nurtured in the choral tradition in the north of England, took part in many competitions and festivals and had only happy experiences of these times. Now retired she wished to play the piano and was well motivated as her daughters had both learned the instrument to Associated Board of the Royal Schools of Music (ABRSM) Grade 8 level. She had a great love of music and was an enthusiastic pupil. At the beginning she was understandably apprehensive as a lady of mature years, but looked forward to and enjoyed the lessons which she found both stimulating and challenging. Within 18 months of commencing she requested taking her first piano examination, Grade 1.

Teacher's objective assessment of pupil's progress prior to entry for Grade 1 examination, autumn term 2008

Mary practises diligently and is making very good progress. Technically she is proficient in her execution of both scales and pieces and enjoys the aural tests. She is of the standard of ABRSM Grade 1 examination.

To enable familiarity with the procedure a 'mock' examination was conducted during a lesson at the teacher's house. At the end of the autumn term she would also perform one of her examination pieces in a pupils' Christmas concert which she was looking forward to immensely. In the weeks immediately preceding her examination she became slightly apprehensive at 'attempting something like this at my age' and the apprehension increased as the date approached (early December). I advised her to play in front of family and friends as often as possible to get used to an audience, which she did; she also played to several pupils from the teacher's practice on a number of occasions and began to feel more comfortable with the ensuing examination.

Outcome of the examination

Mary passed with 113 marks, which is a solid pass; however she viewed it as one of the worst experiences of her life. She was sure that she had failed and felt that she had let me down despite my assuring her that she had not. Although she had passed, her confidence was badly shaken to the extent that she felt unable to play in the Christmas concert or play in front of anyone again, and was definite that she would never take another examination; she was upset and felt annoyed with herself. However, she continued having lessons and gradually over the following 18 months her self-belief increased as she became more confident in her musical abilities and once more thought of playing in front of her family. At this time she also began to think of taking a further examination but felt that she needed psychological help in order to do this. The author (Mary's piano teacher) had now qualified as a hypnotherapist and Mary was given the opportunity to have a therapy session for music performance anxiety (MPA).

Case history: Mary's narrative from the Grade 1 piano examination

In a way I was actually quite looking forward to the piano exam as it would be an achievement at my age. However, on reaching the venue on the day I started to become anxious and especially so in the waiting room seeing the young examinees with their higher grade music. Although the examiner was quite sympathetic, it did not make any difference. My heart was racing and some mistakes in my scales added to my nervousness. My pieces, which I'd been playing fluently and confidently, just seemed to fall apart. I couldn't see the music properly, my hands and fingers were shaking and they didn't seem to belong to me. I was very upset and came out from there and cried. I thought it was a disaster and I'm sure I've failed. It was one of the worst experiences of my life. I never want to play in front of anyone again and feel that I've let you down. I'm never taking another examination and won't play in the Christmas Concert which upsets me as I had been looking forward to this.

Case formulation

Therapist's interpretation and summary

Mary has experienced MPA, which she has never known before; earlier experiences of performances (albeit in a choral setting) had only been happy. Prior to the examination she was positive, enthusiastic, optimistic and a confident pupil. However, post-examination her confidence was badly shaken in all aspects of her performance, with feelings that 'she had let me down'. Her positivity had changed as she now held only negative thoughts regarding her playing of apprehension and anxiety. This affected her self-esteem and had a detrimental effect on her music to the extent that she would no longer perform to anyone (not even her family) and would not take part in the end of term pupils' concert. Her anxiety is preventing her from participating in something that she really wants to do.

Critical analysis: therapist

Mary's narrative highlights the acute cognitive and physiological symptoms of performance anxiety that she experienced during the examination and holds fears that this will recur in a similar situation. Her narration indicates that the nervousness began on reaching the venue, increased in the waiting room and was heightened extensively during the examination, 'I couldn't see the music properly', which is an indication of extreme cognitive anxiety affecting mental perceptions. In fact it has been argued that excessive arousal in performance is the primary cause of a catastrophic decrement during the performance.[1] The therapist believes that this single unfortunate experience of acute cognitive and physiological arousal is continuing to impact on her playing and on her self-belief as a pianist. She experienced extreme anxiety in a specific situation where she felt she was being scrutinised. This can manifest itself as a focal anxiety disorder (see Chapter 6, p. 54); it is said to be a category of anxiety that is a condition that resides in an otherwise healthy functioning individual and is confined to specific situations.[2] There does not appear to be a deep-rooted cause for the acute arousal experienced at this time as there is no history of this in previous performances or in any other areas of her life past or present.

Her negative assessment of one single traumatic experience is preventing her from participating in performances. This is particularly distressing for her as these feelings were unexpected.

Aims and objectives

Mary still holds negative thoughts regarding her ability as a pianist and experiences cognitive anxiety at the thought of a further examination. The negative subjective schemas and emotions which she has held for two years need restructuring into positive perceptions enabling her to view the problem in a more rational way. This will allow for re-assessment of the feared situation in order that it becomes manageable so that she no longer experiences crippling anxiety regarding future performances. In fact it has been argued that cognitive appraisal of a situation is a critical element in defining the subjective stress level of an event or situation.[3] The main objective is to overcome the subjective negativity and maladaptive behaviours. This will allow Mary to feel comfortable once more performing in front of any size audience without experiencing the former crippling somatic symptoms and extreme negative arousal. It is important that she feels in control of the situation and once more looks forward to performing and ultimately taking a further ABRSM examination.

Treatment plan: cognitive hypnotherapy

Cognitive therapy, where the emphasis is on cognitive restructuring of negative thinking patterns, is required. Cognitive therapy targets the negative thoughts and schemas that give rise to maladaptive behaviours,[4] in fact research informs us that negative thoughts lead to self-perceptions of failure and humiliation.[5] However cognitive hypnotherapy (CH), where the individual is in a trance-like state (as in hypnosis) makes this therapy significantly more effective than cognitive therapy as positive thoughts and ideas are being absorbed directly into the unconscious mind.

First (and only) treatment one hour: 15 September 2010

Given the nature of her condition CH was deemed to be the most appropriate treatment for this patient. Mary had no experience of hypnotherapy so an explanation of the process was given at the commencement of the session (see Chapter 2, p. 15).

Mary presented with the following negative schemas (these are her direct quotes):

'I've let myself down'

'I've let others down'

'I'm angry with myself'

'I can't play in front of others'

'I can't believe it happened'

'I can't possibly attempt that again'

Mary's physiological/somatic sensations during the examination were:

shaking hands/fingers;

rapid heartbeat; and

not being able to focus on the music.

Her aspirations for performance were discussed and what would be most important for her in the days preceding and during the performance. Mary chose key words to aid her in performance: *confident*; and *in control*. She also chose a colour to enhance these thoughts. At appropriate times during the therapy the key words were anchored by the therapist on the dominant wrist. At the end of the session she reported feeling very relaxed and happy and much more positive regarding her piano playing. She was looking forward to any future performances to test the effects of the therapy. Mary was given the therapist's *Self-Confidence for Musicians* CD, and was asked to listen to this as often as possible over the subsequent weeks as this would reinforce the therapy. A second appointment was not booked.

Mary's self-assessment of treatment

The Grade 1 experience had completely undermined my self-confidence not only in playing the piano but in any situation where I felt that I was on show and might let myself down. I would just like to point out that prior to the hypnotherapy treatment and the CD I would never in a million years have had confidence to go ahead and take my Grade 2 piano exam and begin preparing for Grade 3. Also I would not have had the confidence to even go to choral auditions, let alone stand on the stage in front of thousands (well, hundreds) of people. I now feel able to travel and go anywhere to sing! I still listen to the CD at times when I am not sure about going somewhere and it helps me to make a positive decision.

(Email, February 2013)

Therapist's assessment of treatment

As Mary was still having weekly piano lessons I was able to assess the efficacy of the treatment on a regular basis. At the first lesson post-treatment she seemed more cheerful and optimistic and her previous confidence seemed to be restored. She has gained new insights into the traumatic experience and the former negative schemas regarding this have been replaced with positivity. After several further lessons, she began enquiring about the Grade 2 piano examination. Her family were encouraging her to take this and Mary felt that 'she would like to have a go'. A single session of cognitive hypnotherapy has changed her outlook on how she views any forthcoming performance.

Researcher's reflections on suitability of treatment

The clinical history of this patient was diagnosed as focal anxiety. Cognitive hypnotherapy was deemed to be the most appropriate treatment which resulted in a beneficial outcome. This case study supports previous research into the use of hypnotherapy for the treatment of anxiety-based conditions, including focal anxiety where there is no deep-seated reason for extreme anxiety. A meta-analysis has been conducted which indicated that using hypnosis as an adjunct to therapy enhances the effectiveness of cognitive-behavioural treatments.[1] Hypnotherapy appears to have been effective for MPA in this instance, both in the short-term and longitudinally. It enabled access to unconscious automated processing allowing for restructuring of unconscious thoughts and feelings. In fact it has been argued that hypnosis and post-hypnotic suggestions can be used to change problem behaviours, dysfunctional cognitions and negative emotions, which can be replaced with positive ideas for desired future behaviour.[6] The post-hypnotic suggestions given during therapy are an important part of the hypnotherapy process and are regarded as a necessary part of the treatment enabling the patient to act upon the suggestions in future experiences.[7] Mary, through cognitive restructuring of one traumatic experience, was once more able to look forward to the performance experience and had regained her former optimism, self-belief and confidence in performance.

It could be argued, however, that cognitive behavioural therapy (CBT) would have been equally as effective as cognitive hypnotherapy. CBT combines psychology, philosophy and behaviour into one comprehensive approach for understanding and overcoming psychological problems; it can be an effective treatment for a number of different conditions, anxiety being one of these.[8] However a meta-analysis examined the efficacy

Appendix 7.1 Log of musical experiences post-therapy treatment

Today's date	Performance date	Performance (e.g. recital/ concert/ informal/exam)	Thoughts/emotions/feelings (positive/neutral/negative)	Physiological symptoms	Post-performance thoughts/feelings (if any)
	28 Jan. 2012	Concert Birmingham town Hall	Very nervous to begin with (on entering venue and taking my place). After first song got into it and felt fine.	Lack of confidence	Felt elated! Wanted to do it all again.
	May 2012	Concert Royal Albert Hall	As above, daunted by the size of the venue.	Very tense	Proud of myself!
	Sept. 2012	Concert Lighthouse, Poole	Overwhelmed to be in the presence of John Rutter.	Had to concentrate so no symptoms!	Again my personal best!
	Jan. 2013	Concert Town Hall Birmingham	Excited and proud to be able to sing in such a great concert.	None really	Well done (I thought!)
	Feb. 2013	Concert Bridgewater Hall Manchester	Same programme as above concert. Brilliant performance. Standing ovations etc. from first note.	Was put on front row which was a bit EEEK! but soon as started to sing felt great.	Brill concert. Best yet.

of psychodynamic therapies for emotional disorders, including anxiety, against CBT and found that the psychodynamic approach was the more effective therapy.[9] The findings from this case study support the beneficial effects of therapies that target both implicit and explicit processes for the reduction of performance anxiety.

Longitudinal outcome

Mary did not need a second therapy and soon began preparing for the ABRSM Grade 2 piano examination, which was taken during the autumn term 2010. She passed with 115 marks (two marks higher than her Grade 1 result). Although still slightly nervous, she reported feeling more positive, and during the examination felt that she was in control of the situation. She experienced none of the previous cognitive or somatic/physiological symptoms. The therapy had been successful in breaking the cycle of negative cognitions caused by the first experience. Mary began preparing for Grade 3 and also at this time joined the Sing Live choral group, which gives concerts at prestigious venues both nationally and internationally. Subsequently she discontinued piano lessons on joining the group as she felt that she was no longer able to give sufficient time to her practice. Appendix 7.1 on page 67 reproduces her log of experiences with Sing Live. This has been included in the book as it is interesting to note that although treatment was given specifically for anxiety in a piano performance this has had a positive impact on her singing performances (albeit in a choral situation).

References

1 Hardy, L., & Parfitt, G. (1991). A catastrophe model of anxiety and performance. *British Journal of Psychology*, *82*(2), 163–178.
2 Stein, M.B., & Stein, D.J. (2008). Social anxiety disorder. *The Lancet*, *371*(9618), 1115–1125.
3 Eysenck, M.W. (1997). *Anxiety and cognition: A unified theory*. Hove: Psychology Press.
4 Kirchner, J.M. (2003). A qualitative inquiry into musical performance anxiety. *Medical Problems of Performing Artists*, *18*, 78–82.
5 Beck, A.T. (1970). Cognitive therapy: Nature and relation to behaviour therapy. *Behavior Therapy*, *1*(2), 184–200.
6 Kirsch, I., Montgomery, G., & Saperstein, G. (1995). Hypnosis as an adjunct to cognitive-behavioral psychotherapy: A meta-analysis. *Journal of Consulting and Clinical Psychology*, *63*, 214–220.

7 Barrios, A.A. (1973). Posthypnotic suggestion in high-order conditioning: A methodological and experimental analysis. *International Journal of Clinical and Experimental Hypnosis, 21,* 32–50.

8 Beck, A.T., & Rush, A.J. (1985). A cognitive model of anxiety formation and anxiety resolution. *Issues in Mental Health Nursing, 7,* 349–365.

9 Shedler, J. (2010). The efficacy of psychodynamic psychotherapy. *American Psychologist, 62*(2), 98–108.

8 Letting others down in clarinet performance

Ghosts from the past

The author deemed it important to include a case study that used both EMDR and CH as a combined treatment. The efficacy of the therapies given in one single session is reported here.

Identifying information

Name:	Sarah
Music performance anxiety:	Clarinet
Gender:	Female
Age:	61 years
Occupation:	Professional musician; peripatetic wood-wind and private teacher

Referral

Sarah contacted me through a colleague who was a fellow musician. She first approached me during the interval of a concert at which she was play-ing when we talked briefly about the anxiety that she was experiencing before and during performance.

Case history: Sarah's narrative from the first treatment session

I am a woodwind teacher of many years' standing and have always felt that I am a competent and successful teacher. I teach clarinet/saxophone/ flute, and my first instrument is the clarinet. I am also first clarinettist in a prestigious amateur orchestra consisting of professional musicians. The orchestra gives four/five concerts each year often having well known professional soloists. I also have other amateur engagements involving ensembles and solo work as well as my instrumental teaching. I never feel anxious when teaching; however I experience exaggerated anxiety when having a solo performance, even if it's only a few phrases, in the ensemble and in the orchestra.

I've had huge performance anxiety for several years but recently it is so bad that on several occasions I've just panicked, I've given excuses and pulled out of playing. At times when I've performed I shake uncontrollably and I know that I'm not giving a good performance. I feel that I'm letting the other musicians down and not showing what I can really do, it's like hiding my light under a bushel. I have a particularly demanding concert on the horizon in several months' time where I have to play a difficult clarinet solo with the orchestra. I know I will feel particularly exposed and I don't want to let the orchestra down. I am already worrying about the forthcoming performance and feeling sick at the mention of it even though it is months away. I know that I am a very good clarinettist and love playing, yet I am not able to overcome my fear of performing in public. I've thought about drugs (beta blockers) and also alcohol to help my confidence; however I've decided that I don't want to follow this route and so I am seeking help.

Both my younger sister and I learned woodwind instruments as children and enjoyed playing and entering competitions without any signs of accompanying anxiety. However when I reached secondary school my father was against my music and I was constantly being told that I should give up my music and concentrate on my academic work. My father had a very domineering personality which made me feel uncomfortable, anxious and panicky when he was around. To a certain extent I was afraid of him, but I loved music and felt that it was something that I did really well, and so was determined to continue. However it got to the stage where I would aim to do the majority of my practice when my father wasn't around to avoid any further confrontations; this situation continued throughout secondary school. My father never encouraged me in any aspect of music and never attended any of my performances even though I was awarded a Diploma of Licentiateship in Clarinet Teaching from a prestigious musical institution.

Case formulation

Therapist's summary and interpretation of Sarah's narrative

There are a number of interesting features in this narrative. First, this experienced musician knows that she is talented with a lot to contribute; however she described her playing in public as 'hiding my light under a bushel'. She is not performing to her optimal level due to her anxiety which begins weeks before a performance. She is prevented from doing the things that she really wants to do: 'on several occasions I've given excuses and pulled out of playing'. The changing nature of the performance setting and the increased attention in solo sections from the other musicians in the orchestra/ensemble cause exaggerated cognitive and somatic anxiety: 'I feel that I am letting other musicians down'. This anxiety in performance was never experienced as a child, when she enjoyed performing.

Critical analysis: therapist

Her narrative indicates that she is suffering from acute music performance anxiety (MPA) in the form of a type of non-generalised social phobia subtype: anxiety experienced only in settings in which the individual is being scrutinised, and reserved for a small number of performance situations.[1] In this instance this specific social phobia subtype manifests itself as a focal anxiety disorder. Although her performance anxiety is severe it is confined to specific situations such as infrequent requirements to play solos as an orchestral section leader; her panic does not occur when playing as a *tutti* clarinettist with the orchestra. She experiences no other significant anxieties in other areas of her life. The possible dynamics underlying this condition are the psychological issues from past experiences which are impacting on her present-day performances.[2] She enjoyed playing and entering competitions as a child 'without any signs of accompanying anxiety'. However as a teenager she was made to feel that academic work was of prime importance, and that music was of no value and should be discontinued. Her father's domineering personality, negativity and lack of encouragement regarding her music caused discomfort and confrontation which resulted in her fear and in her practising when he was absent from home (she hid her talent in order to continue with her music). The therapist/author suggests that this could be a crucial link to Sarah's MPA in her statement 'hiding my light under a bushel'. The lack of support and encouragement throughout secondary school culminating in the non-attendance of her father at the award ceremony of her Licentiateship Diploma also gave a clear message from an important person in her life of the non-importance of her chosen career.

In therapy Sarah presented with the following negative schemas regarding her performance anxiety (direct quotes):

'I'm afraid'

'I'm anxious'

'I can't do what I want to do'

'I'm letting myself down'

'I'm embarrassed'

'I can't control my thoughts'

'It's affecting my sleep'.

Her somatic symptoms of anxiety were:

shaking uncontrollably;

feeling sick;

wanting to go to the toilet constantly;

heightened breathing; and

tension throughout her body (including feet).

Aims and objectives

Sarah has many negative thoughts both weeks before and during concerts. The therapist purports that negative past experiences are impacting on her present day performances causing uncomfortable psychological cognitions both weeks before and during performance, as well as accompanying somatic symptoms of anxiety. The level of cognitive and physiological arousal experienced by this clarinettist is extremely aversive. At the thought of the performance she feels sick months before, and has uncontrollable shaking during the performance. The main aim is to desensitise the past trauma and replace the present cognitive anxiety and uncomfortable emotional feelings with positive thoughts and feelings, enabling her to look forward to performances instead of dreading them. It is argued that the primary emotion of fear can masquerade as anxiety or panic and should these emotions be denied their rightful expression they will persist throughout the lifetime unrelieved.[2]

The main objective is to perform solo in public without the crippling anxiety that she presently experiences and demonstrate her expertise by playing confidently, competently and inspirationally.

Treatment plan: EMDR and CH

First (and only) treatment: 1 November 2010

This patient presented with continuous crippling MPA. The multiple negative domestic experiences, in the therapist's opinion, have played a major role in contributing to this present state. Systematic desensitisation of the traumatic memories through EMDR will be the primary aspect of the overall treatment, followed by CH to reinforce the changed perceptions. Research informs us that a focused emphasis on desensitisation where trauma has existed is a very important component of the overall treatment.[3] The suggestion of a combined therapy was explained carefully by the therapist and Sarah was happy to proceed, although she seemed somewhat sceptical of EMDR.

Eye movement desensitisation and reprocessing

Subjective narrative smoothing had revealed many upsetting episodes involving Sarah's father which became the main targets in EMDR and were collectively rated by Sarah as 8/9 on the SUD scale indicating high trauma. The worst incident was recalled first, during which time she experienced heightened breathing, tension in the shoulders, arms and hands and emotions of anger and fear. Remembrance of specific happenings gradually became more difficult as the most painful memory began to fade. At Sarah's rating of 4/5 on the SUD scale she appeared less anxious, her breathing normalised and the tension in her hands (which she had been gripping tightly) relaxed. She found the memories more difficult to hold and at 0 (the lowest point of anxiety on the scale) she revealed that all the old uncomfortable thoughts and feelings had gone. She now felt, and was aware for the first time that she no longer needed the unfortunate past experiences and could now let them go: 'I have greater insight into what happened and don't need to carry this any longer.' The emotions of anger and fear had completely disappeared and she felt peaceful. She realised that positive things had come out of these experiences; she had been strong and determined and had continued with her music, culminating in the Teacher's Diploma when the easy option would have been to have given up: 'My love of music had given me the strength to continue.' When thinking of future performances Sarah's subjective rating on the VOC scale of 0–7 was 7, the highest level of positivity. 'I now have only positive thoughts and feel happy and euphoric, feelings which I haven't experienced for years.'

Cognitive hypnotherapy

On the completion of EMDR, CH was applied. Prior to trance induction (Chapter 2, p. 15) aspects of her musical performance which were most important to her were discussed: her musicality, interpretation, expertise, memory and connecting with the audience. She linked the emotion of happiness with her breath control and thought of a colour which enhanced this. Her key words, which were anchored during CH, were *competent* and *inspirational*. On completion of hypnotherapy she was given the author's *Self-Confidence for Musicians* audio CD. She was advised to listen to this as often as possible during the first two weeks post-therapy and then as and when she felt the need.

The total duration of the appointment was an hour and thirty minutes. A second appointment was not booked at this time as Sarah wanted to await the outcome of the first session.

Sarah's self-assessment of treatment

As a busy amateur musician I have been experiencing huge perfor-mance anxiety for several years. It was getting so bad that on several occasions I 'chickened out' of playing completely and on others I was shaking uncontrollably and unable to give a good performance. I vis-ited Elizabeth with some degree of scepticism a couple of months prior to an extremely demanding concert. After one session, and listening to the audio recording that she gave me, my whole attitude towards performance changed. I conquered my fear and gave, I am told, a very good confident performance for that concert. Since then I have felt a lot more relaxed and enjoy playing with a new found confidence.

(Testimonial, December 2010)

Therapist's objective assessment of treatment

This participant presented with a social phobia subset manifesting as a specific focal anxiety disorder. Her first negative schema was 'I'm afraid' and anxiety and panic were two emotions that she exhibited prior to per-formances. Therefore given the nature of this case it was deemed by the therapist that the treatment should focus primarily on systematic desensiti-sation of these emotions through EMDR. By being confronted with matters that she had avoided facing it gave her new insights into past problems.

On completion of this a subjective SUD rating of 0 indicated that Sarah's emotions of fear anger and panic had been desensitised, and a VOC rating of 7 showed the highest level of positive thinking. CH using positive imagery and visualisation of performance was used as an adjunct to EMDR and maximised the effects of treatment so that only one session was required.

The desired outcome has been achieved; Sarah no longer holds the former negative schemas, the adverse memories having been desensitised and reprocessed, and replaced with positive cognitions and visualisa-tion. Sarah now feels positive and confident regarding her forthcoming performance and so has not booked a second session. However she has intimated that she will have another treatment if she feels at all 'wobbly' at her next performance.

Researcher's reflections on treatment suitability

Fear is one of the primary emotions, and it can masquerade as anxiety, terror or panic, the three degrees of the intensity of fear. When these emotions are denied their rightful expression they will persist unrelieved.[2] In this case the emotions have been denied their rightful expression, as related in Sarah's narration: 'My father had a very domineering personality which made me feel uncomfortable, anxious and panicky when he was around, to a certain extent I was afraid of him.' In exposure therapy the individual is confronted with the feared situation, person, emotions and past incidents either in imagination or *in vivo*. EMDR has much in common with exposure therapy as the main aspect is confronting or facing a psychotherapeutic problem using systematic desensitisation procedures. Psychotherapy research strategies have confirmed and validated the powerful effects of exposure therapy with certain specific anxiety problems including MPA.[4,5] However there are unique or specific factors attributable to different types of exposure therapies and a number of different techniques may also have resulted in a successful outcome. Exposure *in vivo* creates desensitisation; confronting the feared object or situation reduces the fear so that this is managed or reduced in subsequent exposures.[6] However this form of therapy does not suit everyone; some treatments use virtual reality to help those individuals who experience performance anxiety, as a virtual experience appears less threatening than the real thing.[7]

Flooding and implosion therapies have also reported positive results when applied to different fears and avoidance behaviours.[3] Cognitive behavioural therapy (see Chapter 2, p. 14) similarly encourages the individual to face feared situations and attain mastery of those situations through the use of effective coping strategies. It is argued that all of these behavioural methods based on the exposure paradigm appear to have a common factor operating in the different approaches to the same problem, namely that the individual in some way is confronted with the negative situation and learns that it can be faced without any catastrophic consequences and gradually becomes desensitised.[8]

This case study supports previous research into anxiety-based conditions supporting the therapeutic effects of EMDR.[9–12] The addition of CH in this case is an important adjunct to EMDR. Research informs us that it provides a powerful model for imagery training, conditioning emotional responses, restructuring experiences and directing attention to positive forthcoming experiences.[13] Psychological interventions may be more effective when a combination approach is adopted as it provides added impact and strength to the overall therapeutic effect.[14]

It would appear that a positive effect has been achieved in the above case through EMDR and CH; however through narrative smoothing and uncovering and discussing the historical roots of the disorder the individual gains new insights into past problems. It is believed that uncovering and discussing the original causes of emotional problems is the basis of psychotherapy,[2] and that telling the story to others is one of the essential constituents of our understanding of reality.[15] In some instances this may be all that is needed to effect a cure; the occurrence is more easily understood in the safe environment that the therapist offers. It has also been reported that a portion of patients improve spontaneously without the benefit of psychotherapy.[16]

Longitudinal outcome, April 2014

Sarah did not return for a second therapy as she never felt the need. She still listens to the CD, particularly in the days before an impending concert. She has had several orchestral and ensemble performances since her therapy in 2010 and still maintains her new found confidence and enjoyment in performing. I attended her first concert post-therapy and was amazed at the difference in her playing having listened to her playing in several of the previous concerts. She walked onto the stage confidently and smiling, and when she started playing it was indeed inspirational – one of her key words that she had chosen in hypnotherapy. When playing the clarinet solo it seemed to lift the whole orchestra onto a higher plane, and this was communicated to the audience.

Although she is now living in France, I am still in contact with this musician and follow her progress. She informs me that in the music field she still maintains the beneficial effects of the therapy.

References

1 Turner, S.M., Johnson, M.R., Beidel, D.C., Heiser, N.A., & Lydiard, R.B. (2003). The social thoughts and beliefs scale: A new inventory for assessing cognitions in social phobia. *Psychological Assessment, 15*, 384–391.

2 Barnett, E.A. (1989). *Analytical hypnotherapy: Principles and practice.* Glendale, CA: Westwood Publishing.

3 Garfield, S.L. (2003). Eclectic psychotherapy: A common factors approach. In J.C. Norcross & M.R. Goldfried (eds), *Handbook of psychotherapy integration* (pp. 169–201). New York: Oxford University Press.

4 Orman, E.K. (2003). Effect of virtual reality graded exposure on heart rate and self-reported anxiety levels of performing saxophonists. *Journal of Research in Music Education, 51*(4), 302–315.

5 Orman, E.K. (2004). Effect of virtual reality graded exposure on anxiety levels of performing musicians: A case study. *Journal of Music Therapy, 41*(1), 70–78.

6 Appel, S.S. (1976). Modifying solo performance anxiety in adult pianists. *Journal of Music Therapy, 13*(1), 2–16.

7 Williamon, A., Aufegger, L., & Eiholzer, H. (2014). Simulating and stimulating performance: Introducing distributed simulation to enhance musical learning and performance. *Frontiers in Psychology, 5*(25), 1–9.

8 Lambert, M.J. (2013). Introduction and historical overview. In M.J. Lambert (ed.), *Bergin and Garfield's handbook of psychotherapy and behavior change* (6th edn, pp. 1–85). Hoboken, NJ: Wiley.

9 Arditi, I. (2009). Rafael de Morra: Performance anxiety due to inferiority and cultural difference in 'The Bewitched'. MFA dissertation, York University, Canada.

10 Begley, S. (2009). *The plastic mind*. London: Constable.

11 Doidge, N. (2008). *The brain that changes itself: Stories of personal triumph from the frontiers of brain science*. London: Penguin Books.

12 Swart, I. (2009). The influence of trauma on musicians. DMus thesis, University of Pretoria, Pretoria.

13 Alladin, A. (2008). *Cognitive hypnotherapy: An integrated approach to the treatment of emotional disorders*. Chichester: John Wiley & Sons.

14 Norcross, J.C., & Goldfried, M.R. (eds) (2005). *Handbook of psychotherapy integration* (2nd edn.). New York: Oxford.

15 Butor, M. (1969). *Passing time: A change of heart* (trans. Jean Stewart). New York: Simon & Schuster.

16 Bergin, A.E., & Lambert, M.J. (1978). The evaluation of outcomes in psychotherapy. In S.L. Garfield & A.E. Bergin (eds), *Handbook of psychotherapy and behaviour change: An empirical analysis* (pp. 139–189). New York: Wiley.

9 Trauma when singing in a performance situation
The past need not predict the future

This case is an example of someone who received both EMDR and hypnotherapy for the treatment of music performance anxiety (MPA). However, unlike Sarah (see Chapter 8), two sessions of therapy were required to gain the optimal effect.

Identifying information

Name:	Rebecca
Music performance anxiety:	Voice
Gender:	Female
Age:	41
Occupation:	Mother of two; student with the Open University studying English and music (a pupil from the author's private music practice)

Referral

Rebecca, a singer at an advanced level, began having lessons with me in September 2008 after moving into the area. Her aim was to take the Grade 8 Singing examination (ABRSM) having taken it some years previously with another teacher and failed. She described how she suffered from performance anxiety with which she had been plagued for many years.

Case history: Rebecca's narrative

My mother was a very good amateur singer who had never been allowed to take this to a professional level because of my domineering father. I also felt that I had talent as a singer but my father, an engineer, was against this and wanted me to follow a scientific career as he had done. During my teenage years I resented this, fought against it and continued singing; the result being that my father literally tried to knock it out of me. This caused much anxiety, stress and psychological issues so that in the end I gave up all thoughts of a career in singing, and to please my father concentrated on more academic subjects at school. I became screwed up as I didn't want a scientific career. I failed my A levels and didn't go to university. I feel that all through my life my father had made things worse for me; this was compounded by having a sister who did have a career in science, which pleased my father. Despite not going to university I managed to get a good job in the Foreign Office in London and did well there. At this time I had a boyfriend who was just like my father in his attitude towards me. I finally ended the relationship after four years and thought 'Right, now I am going to sing'; I was aged 24 years.

I had always felt very nervous when performing and always seemed to have the image of my father in the background; I felt that he was judging and criticising me and that I was letting myself down. I was having singing lessons at this time and giving small informal recitals but I was never happy with the outcome; I always felt I fell short of my true potential. I took Grade 8 ABRSM Singing examination but failed quite badly and this felt like the ultimate disaster. Although I was confident practising on my own, I found singing lessons 'nerve racking' and at the examination I just 'fell apart'.

After I moved here and restarted singing lessons I was very interested in taking part in the Christmas concert as your research was close to my heart as I always get very nervous in performance. I was singing in the second half of the concert but felt nervous in the first half and this got worse, and as soon as I started singing my throat felt tense and I had saliva in my mouth which I had to keep swallowing before the long runs, my heart was beating quickly and I could feel my cheeks flushing. Because of all this I felt that I hadn't connected with the audience and was disappointed with my performance. I did enjoy taking part however and being part of the research into music performance anxiety and found it somewhat reassuring that others taking part were also feeling nervous, I wasn't the only one.

Case formulation

Therapist's summary and interpretation of Rebecca's narrative

Important features in this narrative indicate that the domineering personality and the physically abusive behaviour of her father, who was against her musical ambitions, have had far-reaching consequences on Rebecca's singing performances both as a teenager and as an adult. These emotions are so strong in present-day performances that she imagines the spectre of her father while she is performing. The negative criticism that she experienced from her father has affected her self-esteem and self-worth as a musician in spite of her belief that she has talent as a singer. This was compounded by a boyfriend who had a similar attitude as her father towards her regarding her music. She is confident practising on her own where she perceives that she is not being judged; however she experiences both cognitive anxiety and distressing physiological and somatic symptoms of anxiety in a performance or examination situation where she feels she 'falls apart'.

At the public Christmas concert, which formed part of the author's Masters research into music performance anxiety (University of Sheffield), Rebecca's state levels of anxiety (15 minutes prior to her performance) showed a large increase from baseline readings: baseline, 36; pre-performance, 58 (see Chapter 4, p. 36 for the range). Her physiological measurements of blood pressure and pulse rates also increased substantially from her baseline readings. In performance she appeared nervous with flushing of cheeks. She was very interested in taking part in the concert because of the subject matter, as she had continued singing since her Grade 8 examination although she explained to me that she was always very nervous in performance.

Critical analysis: therapist

There are similarities in the historical background of this case with those of Sarah (see Chapter 8, p. 71). An analysis of Rebecca's narrative suggests that she is suffering from social phobia in situations where she feels threatened and under scrutiny, such as a singing examination or a live concert performance. Social phobia, rooted in social anxiety, has been summarised as:[1]

a) Negative cognitions operating in social situations which include fear of negative evaluation, self-consciousness, self-deprecating thoughts and self-blaming attributions for difficulties.
b) Heightened physiological activity.

Rebecca experiences cognitive anxiety as well as physiological and somatic symptoms of anxiety in a performance situation. However, although she experiences destructive and crippling anxiety when performing, this phobic reaction does not occur in other areas of her life and as such it is a form of focal anxiety. The therapist purports that this is as a result of the criticism and physical abuse that she received from her father during her teenage years regarding her ambitions as a singer ('my father literally tried to knock it out of me') and this I believe has had a profound psychological effect on her self-esteem and confidence in her music performances.

In therapy Rebecca presented with the following negative schemas regarding her anxiety (direct quotes):

'I know I'll screw it up'

'I can't control my thoughts'

'I'm hopeless'

'I can't control my emotions'

'I can't control my body'

'I can't control my nerves'.

Physiological and somatic symptoms of anxiety were:

rapid heartbeat;

shaking/ trembling;

tension in throat; and

too much saliva.

Aims and objectives

The problem of anxiety exhibited in performance is inhibiting Rebecca's true potential as a singer; she is unable to move forward in a music performing situation. This is making her feel frustrated and disappointed. The cognitive and physiological/somatic symptoms of anxiety that she finds so distressing heighten the anxiety that she experiences. It has been shown that negative perceptions and images of past trauma exacerbate anxiety in performance.[2] The main aim therefore is to reprocess the dysfunctional perceptions and images, and enhance positive emotions regarding performance. The main objective is to build her self-esteem and self-belief as a talented performer, enabling her to give an assured and confident performance and to enjoy performing without experiencing any of the former negativity.

Treatment plan: EMDR and CH

First treatment (EMDR): 30 May 2010

Rebecca's MPA is complex as it is not related to a single incident but the systematic criticism and physical abuse that she experienced as a teenager, and the verbal disabuse of her singing and possibly a professional career in this domain as an adult. The primary aspect of the overall treatment would be targeting the trauma experienced at this time which in the opinion of the therapist is best addressed initially through EMDR through systematic desensitisation of these experiences.

In therapy the negative criticism and upsetting experiences revealed in Rebecca's narrative regarding her father were the main targets, beginning with the most upsetting incident for her which she rated as 9/10 on the SUD scale. This rating indicates that significant trauma had been experienced at this time. Her most painful negative emotions when recalling this incident were of fear and anger, the strongest physical sensation was tension throughout her whole body which was accompanied by heightened breathing. After fifty minutes of EMDR her rating on the SUD scale decreased to 0, indicating that the negative memories had been desensitised. The negative schemas that she had presented with at the start of treatment had now changed. Where previously she had six negative self-perceptions (four beginning with 'I can't . . .'; see above), post-treatment these had changed into positive perceptions of 'I can . . .'). She no longer thought of herself as being hopeless or that she would 'screw it up'.

Her rating on the VOC scale was 6/7 (7 being the highest level of positivity): negative schemas cited earlier had been reprocessed. Her bodily sensations which she had experienced at the start of therapy when recalling the traumatic memories had now gone completely, her breathing had normalised and she had no tension anywhere in her body. Having targeted and desensitised the most traumatic memories first, the lesser memories of trauma regarding performance when reviewed were more difficult to hold, and no longer caused Rebecca the former anguish or physiological/somatic symptoms of anxiety. If the past has been one of negativity or trauma regarding certain aspects that are important to the individual, the subjective behavioural response to a similar present-day experience will be consistent with the negative affective responses of the past.[3] An adult may experience feelings of fear and being out of control, and will react emotionally and behaviourally accordingly.

Second treatment (CH): 6 June 2010

The second treatment session (one hour) was shorter than the first (90 minutes), the important groundwork having been accomplished in the first session. As the disparate memories had been desensitised and reprocessed in the first session CH should now be beneficial in supporting the reprocessed cognitive perceptions. It should also enhance the positivity achieved in the previous session. Rebecca had experienced hypnotherapy some years previously but it had not been particularly effective. However I explained that it would enhance the EMDR treatment and the combination of the two therapies would strengthen treatment effects. The most important aspects of her singing performance were discussed; she wanted to feel confident, calm and in control in performance, to connect with her audience and feel eager to do more. Her key words, which were 'anchored' on her dominant wrist during hypnotherapy, were *confident, calm* and *in control*; these she felt were the words that would enable her to give her optimum performance. The therapy focused on enhancement of performance and included visualisation of her perfect performance.

On completion of hypnotherapy she was given the therapist's *Self-Confidence for Musicians* CD and advised to listen to this as often as possible, and especially on the day/evening prior to a performance; this would further relax her and add to her confidence. She left feeling happy and relaxed looking forward to her next singing lesson and her next performance.

Rebecca's self-assessment of treatment

> My singing in front of audiences can be adversely affected by pre-performance nerves, which seem to stem from my first solo concerts when I suffered with acute stage fright. The EMDR treatment brought my worst singing nightmares to the surface and I was initially sceptical that anything could be done to help my anxiety when performing, however I came away from the first treatment feeling unburdened as if a weight that I had been carrying around for years had lifted. It was like coming out from underneath a dark cloud. The CH treatment in the second session focused my mind on enjoying singing so that when I performed I was in control and relaxed. It appeared to reinforce everything so that I am now looking forward to performing instead of dreading it.
>
> (Email, June 2010)

Therapist's objective assessment of treatment

Rebecca's past experiences regarding singing performance had been of negativity and trauma which in the therapist's opinion instigated her behavioural response to present-day experiences. In fact it is argued that earlier life experiences elicit a continued pattern of similar affect, behaviour and cognition, the three main constituents of anxiety.[4] Rebecca's negative cognitions and emotions were replaced with positive thoughts and behaviours through cognitive restructuring of dysfunctional memories. Psychological problems were targeted and addressed initially through EMDR and positive cognitions and imagery were reinforced through hypnotherapy, enabling effective treatment outcome in a short space of time.

This case study supports current research into anxiety which suggests that negative affect and beliefs from the past control the individual in the present; however they can be healed quickly, effectively and profoundly when past negative-rooted traumas are changed.[5,6] The negative cognitions and previous perceptions of subjective performance that this patient held have been successfully desensitised and reprocessed in two treatments. Rebecca no longer views performances with dread and apprehension, feels ready to perform and looks forward to being able to give of her best, no longer having the exaggerated anxiety that was previously experienced. In therapy she learned that a small amount of anxiety is natural and does not necessarily herald full-blown MPA: it focuses the mind and can result in an optimal performance as opposed to a large amount of anxiety (which she had experienced) which paralyses the mind.

Researcher's reflections on treatment suitability

EMDR is a very effective treatment for desensitisation of traumatic memories. In fact it is reported that physiological and mental processes are inextricably linked and fear becomes associated with certain stimuli causing a variety of anxiety disorders.[2] By concentrating treatment on the most dysfunctional memories, EMDR targets the actual traumatic event or events together with any flashbacks and nightmare images that elicit the dysfunctional cognitions, emotions or sensations.[7] Rebecca held the image of her father in her mind, always judging her, and this manifested itself most strongly in her performances causing acute anxiety. She had many negative cognitions and memories associated with her ambition to be a singer.

Neurobiological investigations demonstrate that negative/distressing experiences are stored improperly in memory.[8-11] It has been shown that once the negative memories have been identified together with the irrational belief regarding the associative memory, then the process of desensitisation can begin, generally starting with the most powerful memory (the worst time), then the earliest time and the most recent occurrence.[12] In this case study the deep-seated issues resulting from past trauma were effectively desensitised and negative cognitions reprocessed through EMDR. It has been shown that perceived self-efficacy creates a sense of hope,[13] and that expectation of self-efficacy is central to all forms of therapeutic change.[14] The addition of CH enhanced the therapy effects through positive imagery and belief of self-efficacy.

Longitudinal outcome

Rebecca continued to work for her Grade 8 examination and made extremely good progress. She took the examination in the summer term 2010 and passed with a merit award of 126 marks (just four marks below a distinction). I was her accompanist and was in the examination room during the majority of her singing. She was confident before entering the room and this remained with her, she looked relaxed and happy and in control of the situation; there was no sign of the previous heightened anxiety. An important comment on the examiner's mark sheet was that 'overall she gave a convincing and enjoyable performance'.

Rebecca remains in contact and was more than happy to be included in this research as a case study. Since her two treatment sessions in 2010 she has finished an Open University degree and now holds a Masters in Professional Voice Practice. She has also qualified as a neuro-linguistic practitioner and coach, and at the time of her contact with me in March 2017 had just started her own company. In her words, 'it's been full-on here'. She still enjoys performing and has regular engagements singing at weddings and other celebrations. Her dream of becoming a professional musician has been realised.

References

1 Turner, S.M., Beidel, D.C., & Townsley, R.M. (1990). Social phobia: Relationship to shyness. *Behaviour Research and Therapy, 2*, 497–505.
2 Barlow, D.H. (ed.). (2002). *Anxiety and its disorders: The nature and treatment of anxiety and panic* (2nd edn). New York: Guilford Press.
3 Shapiro, F., & Forrest, M.S. (1997). *EMDR: The breakthrough 'eye movement' therapy for overcoming anxiety, stress and trauma*. New York: Basic Books.
4 Aigen, K. (1996). The role of values in qualitative music therapy research. In M. Langenberg, K. Aigen & J. Frommer (eds), *Qualitative research in music therapy: Beginning dialogues* (pp. 9–33). Gilsun, NH: Barcelona Publishers.
5 Shapiro, F. (1995). *Eye movement desensitization and reprocessing: Basic principles, protocols and procedures*. New York: Guilford Press.
6 Shapiro, F. (2002). Paradigms, processing, and personality development. In F. Shapiro (ed.), *EMDR as an integrative psychotherapy approach: Experts of diverse orientations explore the paradigm prism* (pp. 3–26). Washington, DC: American Psychological Association.
7 Shapiro, F. (2007). EMDR and case conceptualization from an adaptive information processing perspective. In F. Shapiro, F.W. Kaslow, & L. Maxfield (eds), *Handbook of EMDR and family therapy processes* (pp. 3–34). Hoboken, NJ: John Wiley & Sons.
8 Siegel, D.J. (2002). The developing mind and the resolution of trauma: Some ideas about information processing and an interpersonal neurobiology

of psychotherapy. In F. Shapiro (ed.), *EMDR as an integrative psychotherapy approach: Experts of diverse orientations explore the paradigm prism* (pp. 85–122). Washington, DC: American Psychological Association.

9 Stickgold, R. (2002). EMDR: A putative neurobiological mechanism of action. *Journal of Clinical Psychology, 58*(1), 61–75.

10 Van der Kolk, B.A. (1996). Trauma and memory. In B.A. van der Kolk, A.C. McFarlane, & L. Weisaeth (eds), *Traumatic stress: The effects of overwhelming experience on mind, body and society* (pp. 279–302). New York: Guilford Press.

11 Van der Kolk, B.A. (2002). Beyond the talking cure: Somatic experience and subcortical imprints in the treatment of trauma. In F. Shapiro (ed.), *EMDR as an integrative psychotherapy approach: Experts of diverse orientations explore the paradigm prism* (pp. 57–84). Washington, DC: American Psychological Association.

12 Luber, M. (2009). *Eye movement desensitization and reprocessing (EMDR) scripted protocols: Basics and special situations.* New York: Springer.

13 Lazarus, A.A. (1973). 'Hypnosis' as a facilitator in behaviour therapy. *International Journal of Clinical and Experimental Hypnosis, 6,* 83–89.

14 Bandura, A. (1977). Self-efficacy: Toward a unifying theory of behavioral change. *Psychological Review, 84*(2), 191–215.

10 Anxiety in the sports arena
The one-incident trigger

Identifying information

Name:	Beth
Anxiety in performance:	Dressage
Gender:	Female
Age:	25 years
Occupation:	Professional horsewoman

Referral

Beth contacted me through my hypnotherapy website regarding performance anxiety before and during dressage competitions.

Case history: Beth's narrative

I had done really well as a young rider and had been awarded various medals. At the age of sixteen I was entered for my first international competition as a junior rider as part of a prestigious team. I was riding a 'sharp pony' that needed very sensitive handling. During my round everything was going well when suddenly the horse went ballistic. I finished the circuit but felt that I had let the team down badly for although they were awarded a medal my round was not included. I continued with my riding after this experience but felt that my confidence had been severely shaken and I was always worried that a similar thing might happen again, although it never did. Although I still took part in competitions I was narrowly missing gold and silver medals and felt that I was letting my family down. I knew in myself that I was a good horsewoman and was capable of winning first prizes, but negative thoughts were always at the forefront of my mind. It's now nine years since this initial experience but when I go into the arena I feel as if I'm looking inward and this is stopping me from achieving my goal.

Case formulation

Therapist's interpretation of Beth's narrative

This narrative indicates that Beth is a capable rider winning medals at a young age and a junior member of a highly prestigious team. She knows that she is a good horsewoman and capable of winning first prizes; however her subjective perception of her capabilities changed radically after the traumatic experience of riding a horse that was suddenly out of control during an important competition. Although it is some years since this incident the psychological effects are still impacting negatively on her present-day performance. Her self-esteem and self-image have been badly shaken as she feels that she has and will continue to let people down (both her team and her family). She has lost confidence in her abilities as a rider and is worried that something similar will happen again.

Critical analysis: therapist

Beth's narrative indicates that she is suffering from acute anxiety on entering the sports arena. However, although her level of performance anxiety in the arena is severe, this is not experienced in other situations (it is confined specifically to the arena, the environment of Beth's initial trauma). The therapist purports that she is experiencing situational anxiety as a focal anxiety disorder as a result of past trauma. In this case focal anxiety is occurring as a result of a specific conditioning experience[1] (see Chapter 6, p. 54). She experiences cognitive anxiety of self-doubt and of being out of control and not living up to the expectations of significant others. Her narrative describes 'looking inward' which is an interesting and revealing comment as it suggests that her mind is still focusing on the negativity of the experience nine years previously. In my opinion this is preventing her from moving forward.

In therapy Beth presented with the following negative schemas regarding her performance (direct quotes):

'I've failed'

'I'm letting myself and other people down'

'I feel rejected'

'I'm embarrassed'

'I'm disappointed'

'I'm inadequate'.

Somatic and cognitive symptoms of anxiety that she experienced in performance were:

shaking/jelly-like feeling;

weak;

exhausted;

heightened breathing;

disorientated;

feelings of not being there; and

shrivelling up, hiding.

Aims and objectives

Beth is experiencing situational or state anxiety when she feels that she is in the spotlight. The negative cognitions and distressing somatic symptoms that she experiences in the arena are strongly inhibiting her performance. It has been suggested that explicit memories of past events can be a prime contributor to situational anxiety.[2] The aim of the therapy therefore is to change the subjective dysfunctional thoughts which appear to originate from one single traumatic experience, enabling Beth to have faith in her ability as a horse woman and once more trust herself. Her critical goals are to be able to perform in the arena feeling in control of the situation, to demonstrate her expertise and competence to both her audience and family members, and to look forward to competitions.

Treatment plan: EMDR and CH

Beth presented with focal anxiety, in the therapist's opinion caused by a single traumatic event. Assessment of the narrative/history strongly suggests that the problems being experienced in the present relate back to this experience. It has been argued that past trauma can cause a psychological reaction resulting in dysfunctional behaviour in a similar present-day situation.[3] If the past event has been one of negativity or trauma, the individual's behavioural response to the present day experience will be consistent with the affective responses of the past.[4] Beth has feelings of fear and not being in control consistent with the experience of the primary trauma. The dysfunctional nature of this memory causes strong feelings of cognitive negativity and distressing physiological/somatic symptoms which are impacting on her performance in the arena. The use of EMDR as the initial treatment should be effective in rapid desensitisation of the trauma. Hypnotherapy can then be used in subsequent treatments as an adjunct to support and enhance positivity.

First treatment (EMDR): 4 March 2013

The procedures of EMDR were explained to Beth and the main target identified (the most traumatic event/experience). She rated this as 10 on the SUD scale, indicating high disturbance (see Chapter 3, pp. 24–25, for theory and protocols). At the commencement of the desensitisation process Beth became very emotional with rapid breathing at recall of the trauma, accompanied by feelings of fear and anxiety. Her strongest negative cognitions were of failure and inadequacy and of letting people down. Bodily sensations were feeling physically sick accompanied by a 'dark feeling'. Once reprocessing had commenced, at her rating of 6 on the SUD she felt 'more peaceful' and could see her father's face looking happy and encouraging her. At 4 her breathing normalised and she appeared far more relaxed. At 3 the negative schemas had been replaced with 'I can see now it wasn't my fault, I wasn't to blame'; at this point the dark feeling had gone. At 0, the greatest desensitisation point, all negative cognitions had disappeared and were replaced with positive subjective thoughts.

Beth could now see that she 'had the guts to carry on', as she had subsequently ridden the horse that had caused the initial trauma for a whole year, the first time being the next day in a competitive situation, with no negative consequences. She felt that the initial trauma was now an acceptable learning curve and that she could at last put this incident behind her. Beth's subjective rating on the VOC scale moved rapidly from 4 to 7, the highest point of positivity where she felt completely 'calm and relaxed' when thinking about the next competition which was the following day. She felt happy and that she could enjoy the performance, and would be able to concentrate on the circuit without any thoughts of worry. She was given the therapist's *Relaxation* CD and asked to listen to this as and when she felt the need. The first appointment had lasted one hour and 30 minutes.

Second treatment (CH): 12 March 2013

At the second treatment session (which lasted one hour), Beth seemed very happy. She had won her competition the day after her previous therapy and she felt elated. She had experienced no negativity and knew that she had proven to herself that she could do it. Beth felt '100% fine with my father' and that he was encouraging and supporting her. He had been at the competition and she sensed that he felt proud of her and her abilities as a horsewoman. A positive effect had been achieved in the first treatment and the addition of CH, when used as an adjunct to EMDR, provides a powerful model of imagery training. In fact research informs us that the use of hypnosis in therapy is a powerful tool for restructuring experiences and directing attention to positive forthcoming experiences.[5] Psychological intervention may be more effective when a combination approach is adopted as it provides added impact and strength to the overall therapeutic effect.[6] In the therapist's opinion hypnotherapy would reinforce Beth's positivity achieved in the previous session, produce optimal results and give peak performance.

As this was her first experience of hypnosis a brief explanation was given regarding the process, followed by a discussion with the therapist where all aspects of her 19 years of training were considered. She talked of the hard work, dedication and sacrifices that she had made in order to reach this high standard, and the many hours of practice that were needed to achieve this. The research literature demonstrates that the mind controls the body.[7] Beth believed in this concept, feeling that for her optimum performance she would need to be mentally relaxed and that this would impact positively on her physiological state. Before trance induction she chose three descriptive words: *confident, focused* and *relaxed*; these became her key words for pre-performance and during the performance, and would be anchored on her wrist during CH at key points. During hypnotherapy visualisation was introduced, Beth seeing herself as a fully accomplished horsewoman in her forthcoming competition and running the whole performance through in her mind from the beginning of the sequence right through to the end. At the end of the second session she was reminded that continued listening to the *Relaxation* CD would be beneficial, especially before competitions. She assured me that she would update me on her future progress.

Beth's assessment of treatment: testimonial

I decided to try hypnosis and EMDR because my performance nerves and anxiety were really starting to affect me in a bad way and ruining my performance. I found Elizabeth's website and I decided to give it a go. I can't thank her enough! After my first treatment I won my competition the next day and after the second treatment I feel fantastic and I am actually enjoying competing again and winning lots – I haven't looked back . . . I can honestly say it was the best thing I ever did.

(Email, May 2013)

Therapist's objective assessment of treatment

Through a combination of EMDR and CH the patient no longer holds her former negative cognitions. The subjective negative schemas have been replaced with a positive mental attitude towards her performance as a horsewoman. The unpleasant bodily sensations have also disappeared so that Beth is now able to concentrate fully on the task at hand. She has faith in her ability, once more trusts herself and now feels confident in entering competitions. Her critical goals, to perform in the arena and give her peak performance demonstrating her expertise and competence (to both her audience and family members) have been achieved. She is now able to look forward to competitions rather than dreading them.

Researcher's reflections on treatment suitability

The literature provides evidence of the interrelationship between cognitive, physiological and behavioural aspects of anxiety and how these impact on performance.[8] The interventions used in this case study addressed the strong relationship between cognitive arousal and emotions and the explicit role that memory plays as a key component of anxiety. However it could be argued that cognitive behavioural therapy (CBT) might have produced a similar result. CBT has generated much interest in the treatment of psychological problems in the realm of sport and there is a developed literature verifying this.[9–12] This intervention, when used in the field of sport, is aimed to improve performance and involves positive self-talk and goal-setting. It is designed to activate mental processes to change existing thought patterns in an attempt to influence the occurrence of a desired action or behaviour.[13] However although positive effects have been reported in the area of the cognitive therapies, a large number of sessions are usually required (10 or more) and core problems are not treated.

In fact it has been argued that there is increasing concern regarding the relapse rate at follow-up sessions for those individuals who have undergone symptom-based cognitive behavioural treatment.[14] Research has shown that when hypnosis is used as an adjunct to CBT, five 90-minute sessions were significantly more effective in reducing the symptoms of acute stress disorder than CBT alone.[15] However, when choosing interventions for individuals with specific problems in any area practitioners should always consider the following: *what* treatment is most effective for *this* individual with *that* specific problem and under *which* set of circumstances?[16] In the case study reported here EMDR was directed at the initial trauma and was followed by CH in the subsequent session, where the emphasis was on enhanced attention, self-confidence, positive visualisation and goal-setting in performance. The combination of the two therapies was extremely effective for the reduction of sports anxiety in this case, instigating a quick resolution to the problem of sports anxiety.

Longitudinal outcome

Beth still keeps in touch to update me on her progress.

May 2013

Beth has won every competition she has entered since her treatments. An article about her horse riding and successful dressage competitions has appeared in a prestigious equestrian magazine.

June 2013

She has been filmed for a television programme which followed her activities with horses throughout her day.

References

1 Stein, M.B., & Stein, D.J. (2008). Social anxiety disorder. *The Lancet, 371*(9618), 1115–1125.
2 Wills, F. (2009). *Beck's cognitive therapy*. Hove: Routledge.
3 Aigen, K. (1996). The role of values in qualitative music therapy research. In M. Langenberg, K. Aigen & J. Frommer (eds), *Qualitative research in music therapy: Beginning dialogues* (pp. 9–33). Gilsun, NH: Barcelona Publishers.
4 Shapiro, F., & Forrest, M.S. (1997). *EMDR: The breakthrough 'eye movement' therapy for overcoming anxiety, stress and trauma*. New York: Basic Books.
5 Alladin, A. (2008). *Cognitive hypnotherapy: An integrated approach to the treatment of emotional disorders*. Chichester: John Wiley & Sons.
6 Norcross, J.C. & Goldfried, M.R. (eds) (2005). *Handbook of psychotherapy integration* (2nd edn.). New York: Oxford.
7 Wolfe, B.E. (2005). *Understanding and treating anxiety disorders: An integrative approach to healing the wounded self*. Washington, DC: American Psychological Association.
8 Kenny, D.T. (2010). The role of negative emotions in performance anxiety. In P.N. Juslin & J.A. Sloboda (eds), *Handbook of music and emotion: Theory, research, applications* (pp. 425–451). New York: Oxford University Press.
9 Landin, D., & Herbert, E. P. (1999). The influence of self-talk on the performance of skilled female tennis players. *Journal of Applied Sport Psychology, 11*, 263–282.
10 Locke, E.A. (1991). Problems with goal-setting research in sports – and their solution. *Journal of Sport and Exercise Psychology, 13*, 311–316.

11 Luiselli, J.K., & Reed, D.D (2011). *Behavioral sport psychology: Evidence-based approaches to performance enhancement.* New York: Springer-Verlag.
12 Smith, A.M., Maragos, A., & van Dyke, A. (2000). Psychology of the musician. In R. Tubiana & C.P. Amadio (eds), *Medical problems of the instrumentalist musician* (pp. 135–170). London: Martin Dunitz.
13 Johnson, J.J.M., Hrycaiko, D.W., Johnson, G.V., & Halas, J.M. (2004). Self-talk and female youth soccer performance. *The Sport Psychologist, 18,* 44–59.
14 Kenny, D.T. (2011). *The psychology of music performance anxiety.* Oxford: Oxford University Press.
15 Bryant, R., Moulds, M.L., Guthrie, R., & Nixon, R. (2005). The additive benefit of hypnosis and cognitive-behavioral therapy in treating acute stress disorder. *Journal of Consulting and Clinical Psychology, 73,* 334–340.
16 Paul, G.L. (1967). Strategy of outcome research in psychotherapy. *Journal of Consulting Psychology, 31*(2), 109–118.

11 IBS and anxiety at work and in the sports arena

A life-changing experience post-therapy

Identifying information

Name:	Penny
Anxiety:	Manifesting itself in various ways and situations
Gender:	Female
Age:	47 years
Occupation:	Child psychologist

Referral

Penny contacted me via my website as she had heard that individuals with chronic irritable bowel syndrome (IBS) had been helped and supported by having hypnotherapy. This condition was impacting negatively on different important areas of her life and medical intervention of drugs over a number of years had failed to alleviate the symptoms.

Case history: Penny's narrative

I often feel anxious in all sorts of situations and I'm permanently anxious at work (apart from holidays). It's got so bad that I can't use the phone at work as I'm afraid of letting myself down, but others have a vision of me as a strong person. When dealing with adults in my job I get very anxious. Dad left home when I was six months old and mum remarried. My stepfather was a very flat, unemotional man and not at all sociable. My elder sister was always the needy, favoured one, wanting and getting my mother's attention, so I was always the good daughter as I never wanted to give mum any stress and craved her attention. I've never got on well with my sister and growing up she would make me feel that I was stupid, ugly, and awkward, so I was always worried about getting things wrong, yet mum seemed to favour her. I felt isolated from both of them. I have been married four times and have three sons, and for the last 15–20 years I have suffered daily from IBS and it is ruling my life. I am not a very confident person anyway and this is adding to the anxiety that I already feel. It's affecting my social/pleasure activities. I love horse riding and do this on a regular basis and take part in small competitions which involves dressage, show jumping and cross country. I feel scared before these events anyway as I always want to achieve success and not let myself down, and having the IBS hanging over me makes it much worse. The symptoms are much stronger just before and during the competition, so I have to take extra medication to help this. I really love riding and would love to achieve success without feelings of panic or catastrophising.

Case formulation

Therapist's interpretation of Penny's narrative

There are many interesting features here. The primary area of Penny's concern is the chronic IBS with which she has suffered for many years and which is markedly affecting the quality of her life. However of equal concern is the anxiety she experiences in the workplace on a daily basis, and her heightened performance anxiety when taking part in horse riding competitions. Her lack of confidence adds to her negativity both in her work and leisure pursuits where she is afraid of letting herself down and has the added stress of maintaining a strong persona: 'others have a vision of me as a strong person'. The unsettled childhood, her father having left home when she was six months, together with her dysfunctional relationship with her sister and mother, caused feelings of isolation. The negative experiences in her formative years would appear to be impacting on her present life and could be the root cause of her chronic anxiety: she says 'I often feel anxious in all sorts of situations' and she is permanently anxious at work. Her many dysfunctional experiences could also be the underlying cause of her IBS.

Critical analysis: therapist

IBS has a strong female predominance and is characterised by chronic abdominal pain or discomfort associated with disordered bowel habit. It is a condition which is far from trivial and accounts for 40% of all consultations in the UK in secondary care. In fact it accounts for a substantial absence from work in the population as a whole.[1,2] We are informed that anxiety is more common in IBS sufferers than in the general population and although medication is given to alleviate pain and anxiety (as in this case) the symptoms still persist. It has been reported that IBS patients are more anxious than healthy controls, showing greater anxiety and depression;[3] they also show a greater lifetime incidence of treatment for anxiety.[4] However it could be argued that the condition of IBS itself compounds anxiety. Treatments can be divided into dietary and lifestyle modifications, psychological treatments and drug therapy.[5]

A careful diagnosis of Penny's case history indicates that her anxiety has been instigated by an accumulation of negative past experiences which have resulted in chronic IBS which has not responded to pharmaceutical drugs. Causation factors of the presenting symptoms (both cognitive anxiety and IBS) appear to be deep rooted and multifarious. This can be contrasted with Beth (see Chapter 10, p. 89) where performance anxiety in the sports arena was instigated by one specific traumatic experience. Research has demonstrated that psychotherapy may benefit those patients with chronic disabling symptoms resulting from IBS who are resistant to conventional treatment,[6] and that hypnotherapy and relaxation therapy have been effective in randomised trials. Hypnotherapy in particular has been shown to produce a long-lasting benefit.[7]

In therapy Penny presented with the following subjective negative schemas (direct quotes):

'I have low self-esteem'

'I feel stupid, awkward, ugly'

'I feel unfeminine'

'I feel excluded, different, an outsider'

'I constantly worry I'll get things wrong'

'I don't fit in'

'I'm indecisive'

'I don't know how to deal with situations'

'I can't cope but I mustn't let people down, I don't want them to see'.

Emotions experienced were:

angry;

scared;

isolated;

sad; and

disappointed.

Somatic symptoms of anxiety experienced in performance were:

heaviness in upper chest;

tightness around diaphragm; and

heightened breathing.

Aims and objectives

Penny is experiencing chronic anxiety which is exacerbated by her diag-nosed medical condition, IBS. The anxiety is affecting her in the workplace where she is constantly worrying, but is also affecting her leisure/sports activities. She has many subjective negative schemas which the therapist believes are the result of the past dysfunctional experiences. The main aim of the therapy therefore is to replace the cognitive negativity with more positive constructive thoughts and enhance self-esteem. The main objec-tive is the eradication of the symptoms of IBS. Further objectives are to increase her subjective confidence in the work place and in the perfor-mance arena so that she no longer experiences the crippling inhibiting anxiety that she has lived with for so many years and can achieve her full potential without catastrophising.

Treatment plan: EMDR followed by CH

An assessment of Penny's narrative indicates that the negative experiences and dysfunctional relationship that she appears to have with her mother and sister could be the root cause of both her IBS and chronic anxiety syndrome. Targeting and desensitising the initial traumas should have a beneficial effect in all other important areas in her life: the IBS, her anxiety in the work-place and her performance anxiety in the sports arena.

It has been suggested that when a distressing experience results in per-sistent anxiety, the information processing system in the brain has stored the experience without adequately processing it to an adaptive resolution. The event is 'frozen in time' in the moment of fear and pain and this lays the foundation for future inappropriate dysfunctional responses to similar events.[8] When subjective implicit memories have not been processed this may be at the root of a variety of psychological issues in the present.[9,8] Emotions, sensations and perspectives of earlier events colour the perceived view of similar present-day events; a current situation similar to an earlier event will automatically link into the memory network in which the earlier event is stored.[10] The image of the experience activates the aspect of memory held in the occipital cortex, which controls visual images in the brain and can also elicit both sounds and smells connected to the experience.[11] The procedures in EMDR have been developed to identify, access and target dysfunctionally stored experiences and to stimulate the innate processing system, which allows adaptive resolution of the information and shifts the information to the appropriate memory systems.[12,13] Pinpointing the target (the traumatic experience) and reprocessing the disparate memory is crucial in the initial stages of EMDR treatment.

Once this primary aim has been achieved (and this may take a number of sessions), the application of hypnotherapy, as an adjunct to EMDR, should enhance overall therapy outcome. It is believed that hypnosis enables access to unconscious psychological processing when the critical faculty of the conscious mind is bypassed during a trance-like state.[14] It can also be used as a means of empowerment in new and creative ways;[15] post-hypnotic suggestions are an important part of therapy and are used to shape desired future behaviour.[16] Freudian theory states that we tend to repress memories associated with negative experiences; a major component of his theory is that the ego defends itself from anxiety by repression of potentially threatening memories.[17] This general theory of forgetting has received little support; however it has now become influential in the treatment of certain clinical conditions such as disorders arising from trauma and anxiety.[18]

First treatment: 25 September 2014

The first session (of one hour 30 minutes) began with a thorough investigation of Penny's history, including the most distressing present-day symptoms of anxiety and situations which exacerbate these. To formulate the most effective therapy for the patient it is crucial to gather, formulate and use the material in such a way to obtain optimal outcome of treatment.

EMDR

This was deemed to be the most effective treatment by the therapist with which to commence treatment and an explanation of the process was duly given. There were many upsetting incidents in Penny's history but the most traumatic, experienced at a young age, was the initial target in therapy. When revisiting this trauma and the associative disparate memories, she rated this as 9 on the SUD scale. Her cognitions were of feeling stupid, worried, wanting to hide, and feelings of isolation. The main emotions were of being really scared and anxious; somatic (bodily) sensations were feelings of tightness around the diaphragm and heightened breathing. As the indecisive memories were gradually desensitised Penny noted a reduction on the SUD scale so that at 3 the tightness in her chest had changed to a 'warm feeling' and the breathing had normalised. At 1 her negative perceptions of the experience had changed so that she felt 'happy and OK' which was reflected reciprocally on the VOC scale where she rated her positive perceptions of the experience as a 6 (the highest positivity on the scale is 7). At this point she felt 'safe, confident and independent' with feelings that she could look after herself. She was given the therapist's *Relaxation* CD and was asked to listen to this if she experienced any feelings of anxiety between the sessions.

Second treatment (EMDR): 14 October 2014

Penny reported back that her husband had noticed that she was 'more chilled' after the first session and that this had continued throughout the ensuing weeks. The second session (of one hour 30 minutes again) concentrated on desensitisation of early disparate memories in childhood. This focused on the relationship with her mother and sister where she felt that her mother loved and favoured her sister more than her and no matter how hard she tried she couldn't gain her mother's love and support. There were a number of incidents that were similar in content and this conglomeration of experiences she rated as a 9/10 on the SUD. Her negative cognitions were that she felt excluded, different, an outsider. The emotions were of sadness, anger, concern 'that she would get things wrong', feeling stupid, unloved, and 'not wanting her sister to be there'. The primary somatic symptom was one of heaviness in the upper chest. The ideal positive perception for Penny was that she survived, she was strong, and could be independent and self-assured; however prior to desensitisation her belief in this was at the bottom of the VOC scale at 0.

As the session progressed the disparate memories became less upsetting through the desensitisation process and at her rating of 6 on the SUD scale her perceptions had changed to feelings of disappointment with her mother for not appreciating her as she had always worked harder than her sister but was never given the attention that she deserved. At the lowest level of disturbance – her rating of 0 on the scale – Penny felt really good and that she was strong and had survived all the early traumas of childhood. Her perception of her sister had changed so that she now felt that her sister was weak and pathetic. Her positive assessment on the VOC scale at the end of the session was 7 (the highest level). She could see that she was continually better than her sister and it was her sister that couldn't cope. Her feelings of anger and sadness had now disappeared and she no longer felt an outsider, excluded or different. When checking on the somatic feelings that she had experienced at the start of the EMDR treatment, the heaviness in the upper chest felt lighter.

Third treatment (EMDR): 23 October 2014

Penny reported that she had a good effect after the last session, had less negative cognitions, and had been reminding herself of all the positives. The third treatment (of one hour 30 minutes) concentrated on her driving test at age 17. She had passed the test at the first attempt and was pleased with herself. However, she had a negative reaction from her mother, which belittled her success and had upset Penny greatly at the time. She was told by her mother to keep it a secret so that it would not upset her sister. She was convinced then that no matter how hard she tried to please her mother, her sister was still the favoured one.

This incident was rated as 5/6 on the disturbance scale, so although not high trauma it still evoked negative feelings of not being important, being unwanted and second best. The main emotions were apprehension, feeling anxious and disappointment. When recalling the incident she experienced heightened breathing. Desensitisation of the disparate memories lowered the rating of disturbance to 1 where she felt that that this incident was no longer important. The positive rating on the VOC increased from the initial 0 (prior to desensitisation) to 7, the highest subjective rating. At this point in therapy her perceptions had changed so that she was aware that the negative experiences were not her fault and she felt 'brave, self-sufficient and decisive'.

Fourth treatment (hypnotherapy): 20 November 2014

It was almost a month since I had treated Penny and the positive effect from therapy was continuing. She was feeling quite upbeat about things: although as yet we had not looked specifically at her anxiety in the workplace, she reported that she was feeling less anxious and more confident and her IBS symptoms were not as evident. However, in the sports arena, although she was 'more chilled' in the days before competitions, she still took double the amount of prescription drugs for IBS the night before to ensure getting through the different stages of the competition without pain or embarrassment.

Hypnotherapy treatment (a session of one hour 15 minutes) was directed at changing the subjective negative perceptions both in the workplace and in riding competitions.

As Penny had not experienced hypnotherapy previously the process was explained to her. Although feeling less anxious at work she still had feelings of apprehension when dealing with adults and wanted to feel more confident in this area. Her prime concern at this session, however, was the anxiety she experienced when riding which included dressage, show jumping and cross country. She wanted to feel 'confident, brave and excited' when taking part in competitions and these became her 'key words' in hypnotherapy. She described how at 12 years of age when she first began riding she had no nerves; however she gradually became more anxious so that she became 'scared' of competitions, and in her mid-twenties the IBS started which made things worse.

She agreed that the key words that she had chosen would be suitable for both the workplace and riding competitions. After the trance induction, hypnotherapy consisted of positive visualisation of situations at work where she had previously felt uneasy, and seeing herself as she wanted to be, feeling confident in all situations. Likewise the anxiety she experienced in riding was directed towards positive goals and visualisation not only during the competition but in the days pre-, during and post-competition. Most important to her was self-organisation prior to the competition and being 'in the right place at the right time', feeling ready, organised and without catastrophising. Her aim was to allow herself to make mistakes and to feel 'OK' about that. Her three key words were *confident, brave* and *excited* and they were applied to her dominant wrist at specific times during therapy to reinforce how she wanted to feel, and post-hypnotic suggestions given during the trance state (to be acted on in the conscious state) enhanced the positivity.

Fifth (and last) treatment (hypnotherapy): 30 January 2015

It had been two months since Penny's previous treatment and she reported that her IBS had improved greatly. This had impacted positively on her self-perception in the workplace as she felt more comfortable and confident in her abilities to deal with any problems that arose without the previous feelings of tension and dread. She also reported feeling less anxious and apprehensive in the days leading up to competitions. Previous to the therapy sessions she had always loved planning the times for the three different stages: dressage, show jumping and cross country but in spite of meticulous planning, changing the equipment for each stage would cause feelings of panic and catastrophising. Since the previous therapy session she had competed in one competition and had felt much more confident and relaxed about the whole thing. Her self-esteem had improved greatly; she felt that if she did her best she could allow herself to make mistakes, and that it didn't really matter. At this competition she experienced no panic or catastrophising at any of the three different stages in the competition. She was a little nervous in the dressage arena with the closeness of the audience, but seeing familiar faces added to her confidence and excitement as she wanted to show what she knew she was capable of. Previously she had felt more uncomfortable with known audience members as she thought that she had to live up to everyone's expectation of her.

The remainder of the session (which lasted for one hour in total) was taken up with further hypnotherapy, reinforcing all the positive suggestions and imagery instilled in the previous session as treatment effects are usually stronger during a second session of hypnotherapy. When hypnotherapy has not been experienced previously it is more beneficial to the client to have two or more sessions as sometimes the client is resistant (they perceive losing control) and therefore the deepest state of trance is not always realised. Trance state usually becomes deeper with each subsequent session as the client becomes more at ease and familiar with this (they know the procedure).

Penny's assessment of treatment: testimonial

> For the last 15–20 years I have suffered daily with IBS. It was ruling my life and adding to the anxiety that I often felt anyway. I tried counselling, cognitive behavioural therapy (CBT) and my GP referred me to the hospital for tests on a number of occasions but this showed up nothing. Trawling the internet in desperation I read a number of stories where people had been supported with IBS by having hypnotherapy. I decided anything was worth a try. I had EMDR and hypnotherapy and have been amazed that after only a few sessions I was symptom-free and feeling far more confident in my life. I wish I had done this years ago, and that my GP had discussed it as an option. This has made such a difference to me; you really don't have to live with IBS.
>
> (Testimonial, February 2015)

Therapist's objective assessment of treatment

The joint therapies adopted for this patient have given a positive outcome. The main goal of being free of the distressing symptoms of IBS has been achieved and this has had a beneficial effect in other areas of Penny's life. There is no doubt that this condition exacerbated her anxiety and lack of confidence both in the workplace and the sports arena. However this patient had experienced multiple incidents of trauma both as a child and as a teenager.

It was therefore of prime importance that the root cause of the anxiety (which can be posited ultimately led to chronic IBS) was addressed first through EMDR. Having targeted, desensitised and reprocessed these experiences, her self-perceptions changed, her chronic anxiety was lessened considerably and her somatic symptoms of anxiety (IBS) dissipated. After the first session of hypnotherapy, cognitive symptoms of anxiety both at work and in the sports field were reduced considerably. Her self-esteem was restored, the former negativity had gone, she felt confident and able to do the things that she loved (riding) without the former crippling anxiety. It has been argued that a trance state provides a special psychological state in which the patient reassociates and reorganises inner psychological complexities using their own capacities in accordance with their own life experiences.[14]

Researcher's reflections on treatment suitability

There is accumulating evidence from the literature that psychodynamic psychotherapy is effective for the treatment of emotional conditions, particularly anxiety and related conditions, where the primary focus of the therapy session is on affect and the expression of emotion.[19,20] This is not surprising as the psychodynamic therapies focus on the root cause of the problem as opposed to the focus being on the presenting symptoms (therefore working from the bottom up). For nearly half of this individual's life she has been plagued with IBS. Her experience would appear to be a classic example of how the mind affects the body.

It has been argued that emotions and the ensuing behaviour are dependent on cognitive processing.[21] However subsequent studies have noted the importance of considering the context in which the behaviour first occurred: relationships with significant others, determinants of behaviour and the underlying aetiology of the symptoms.[22] Investigative research shows that emotional processing often occurs outside conscious awareness and produces a fast, involuntary, autonomic response and guides decision making.[23] It is argued that processes no longer in conscious awareness produce automatic responses that are not governed by the individual on a conscious level, and are implicit.[24] EMDR and hypnotherapy address both conscious and unconscious memories, explicit and implicit. Implicit processes, aspects of trauma experienced of which the individual is no longer consciously aware, would appear to be the underlying factor of the medical condition and the accompanying anxiety reported here. The importance of addressing both implicit (not remembered) and explicit (remembered) memories respectively have been shown and have resolved the issues related to this complex case history.

Longitudinal outcome

I received an email from Penny in 2017. She had experienced a distressing year with her horses, with one sudden death and having to retire another horse. Compounding this, she had a riding accident and suffered a broken shoulder, which needed surgery. This had caused numerous problems, so she had not competed for a while; however, she had just bought another horse and felt that she would soon be ready to start competing again. Penny still found that her IBS symptoms were greatly reduced and that she was able to deal with any residual anxiety in different areas of her life using the techniques that she had been taught in therapy. In her own words: 'at the moment I don't feel the need for a top-up therapy'.

References

1　Longstreth, G.F., Wilson A., Knight, K., et al. (2003). Irritable bowel syndrome, health care use, costs: a U.S. managed care perspective. *American Journal of Gastroenterology, 98*, 600–607.

2　Wells, N.A., Hahn, B.A., & Whorell, P.J. (1997). Clinical economics review: irritable bowel syndrome. *Alimentary Pharmacology and Therapeutics, 11*, 1019–1030.

3　Henningsen, P., Zimmerman, T., & Sattel, H. (2003). Medically unexplained physical symptoms, anxiety, and depression: A meta-analytic review. *Psychosomatic Medicine, 65*, 528–533.

4　Walker, E.A., Katon, W.J., Jemelka, R.P., & Roy-Byrne, P.P. (1992). Comorbidity of gastrointestinal complaints, depression, and anxiety in the Epidemiologic Catchment Area (ECA) Study. *American Journal of Medicine, 92*, 26S–30S.

5　Spiller, R.C. (2005). Irritable bowel syndrome. *British Medical Bulletin, 72*(1), 15–29.

6　Guthrie, E., Creed, F., Dawson, D., & Tomenson, B.A. (1993). A randomised control trial of psychotherapy in patients with refractory irritable bowel syndrome. *British Journal of Psychiatry, 163*, 315–321.

7　Houghton, L.A., Atkinson, W., Whitaker, R.P., Whorell, P.J., & Rimmer, M.J. (2003). Increased platelet depleted plasma 5-hydroxytryptamine concentration following meal ingestion in symptomatic female subjects with diarrhoea-predominant irritable bowel syndrome. *Gut, 52*, 663–670.

8　Shapiro, F. (2001). *Eye movement desensitization and reprocessing: Basic principles, protocols and procedures* (2nd edn.). New York: Guilford Press.

9　Baddeley, A.D. (1999). *Essentials of human memory.* Hove: Psychology Press.

10　Shapiro, F. (2007). EMDR and case conceptualization from an adaptive information processing perspective. In F. Shapiro, F.W. Kaslow & L. Maxfield (eds), *Handbook of EMDR and family therapy processes* (pp. 3–34). Hoboken, NJ: John Wiley & Sons.

11 Grand, D. (2003). *Emotional healing at warp speed: The power of EMDR*. New York: Present Tents Publishing.

12 Siegel, D.J. (2002). The developing mind and the resolution of trauma: Some ideas about information processing and an interpersonal neurobiology of psychotherapy. In F. Shapiro (ed.), *EMDR as an integrative psychotherapy approach: Experts of diverse orientations explore the paradigm prism* (pp. 85–122). Washington, DC: American Psychological Association.

13 Stickgold, R. (2002). EMDR: A putative neurobiological mechanism of action. *Journal of Clinical Psychology, 58*(1), 61–75.

14 Rossi, E.L., & Cheek, D.B. (1994). *Mind–body therapy: Methods of ideodynamic healing in hypnosis*. New York: W.W. Norton.

15 Blenkiron, P. (2005). Stories and analogies in cognitive behaviour therapy: A clinical review. *Behavioural and Cognitive Psychotherapy, 33*, 45–59.

16 Barrios, A.A. (1973). Posthypnotic suggestion in high-order conditioning: A methodological and experimental analysis. *International Journal of Clinical and Experimental Hypnosis, 21*, 32–50.

17 Freud, S. (1962). The ego and the id. In J. Strachey (ed.), *The standard edition of the complete psychological works of Sigmund Freud*, vol. *XIX* (pp. 3–62). New York: W.W. Norton.

18 Baddeley, A.D., Eysenck, M.W., & Anderson, M.C. (2009). *Memory*. Hove: Psychology Press.

19 Shedler, J. (2010). The efficacy of psychodynamic psychotherapy. *American Psychologist, 62*(2), 98–108.

20 Westen, D., & Morrison, K. (2001). A multidimensional meta-analysis of treatments for depression, panic, and generalized anxiety disorder: An empirical examination of the status of empirically supported techniques. *Journal of Consulting and Clinical Psychology, 69*(6), 875–899.

21 LeDoux, J. (1993). Cognition versus emotion, again – this time in the brain: A response to Parrott and Schulkin. *Cognition and Emotion, 7*(1), 61–64.

22 Spitzer, R.L., & Wakefield, J.C. (1999). DSM-IV diagnostic criterion for clinical significance: Does it help solve the false positives problem? *American Journal of Psychiatry, 156*(12), 1856–1864.

23 Dvorak-Bertsch, J.D., Curtin, J.J., Rubinstein, T.J., & Newman, J.P. (2007). Anxiety moderates the interplay between cognitive and affective processing. *Psychological Science, 18*(8), 699–705.

24 LeDoux, J. (1989). Cognitive-emotional interactions in the brain. *Cognition and Emotion, 3*, 267–289.

12 Confidence in presentations

Hypnotherapy makes it so

Identifying information

Name:	Craig
Anxiety in the work place:	Presentations and meetings
Gender:	Male
Age:	29
Occupation:	Managing consultant
Referral:	Through the Hypnotherapy Register

Craig's narrative

I wasn't that interested in school but at university I worked hard and did well and was lucky in the jobs I applied for. I found that I was good at speaking and enjoyed this aspect of my work. I have been in the same job now for a number of years and have several people working for me. In the day to day things at work I'm fine and I think I come over as being competent and someone that knows what he is doing and being a confident person; however if something significant arises such as important meetings or a presentation that I would have to give with a critical audience then I start to panic. This has been happening over the last year or so after an important meeting with significant others where I just fell apart. I lost my train of thought and felt that I couldn't speak, my mind just went completely blank and I wanted the ground to open up and swallow me. After an embarrassing few minutes I walked out of the meeting it; felt like a panic attack. Although nothing like this has happened since I am always worried that it could happen again and I have an important presentation on the horizon which I want to feel really confident about. I can't remember any specific trauma in the past that may have caused this panic which makes it quite frightening, as I keep thinking if it's happened once it can happen again.

Case formulation

Therapist's interpretation of Craig's narrative

Craig appears to be suffering from performance anxiety in the workplace. His anxiety is not a generalised fear but a form of focal anxiety which is domain-specific experienced in situations which are highly important to him (see Chapters 6–8). He describes acute symptoms of cognitive anxiety ('I lost my train of thought and felt that I couldn't speak'), as well as physiological/somatic symptoms ('it felt like a panic attack') while speaking in an important meeting. It would appear that the worry and anxiety that he experiences now when thinking about future presentations/meetings has been triggered by this one unfortunate experience. It is interesting that until this meeting there was no indication of the subsequent performance anxiety and no past incident that this could possibly be related to.

Critical analysis: therapist

In therapy Craig presented with the following negative schemas regarding the traumatic meeting (direct quotes):

'I was pathetic'

'I felt shocked and was disbelieving that it was happening'

'I was embarrassed and felt helpless'

'I let myself down'.

However, during the consultation it transpired that he had not done enough preparation for this particular meeting, and had been somewhat blasé and too laid-back about the whole thing. He felt that his previous positive experiences had prevented him from consciously anticipating difficult questions, looking fully at the objectives and understanding what was required. It would appear that the main causation factor of the performance anxiety could in fact be over-confidence in his abilities and experience, and hence his lack of preparation. Such lack of preparation has been shown to be a key element in causing cognitive dysfunction in performance; in fact it has been argued that being unprepared heightens anxiety and exacerbates nervous thoughts.[1] Cognitive appraisal of a situation is a critical element in defining the subjective stress level of an event or situation,[2] and when cognition is affected in performance the resultant conditions are loss of concentration, heightened distractibility, memory failure and maladaptive cognitions.[3] Craig's experience was a worst-case scenario leading to a complete breakdown of performance resulting in a hasty exit from the performance scene.

Aims and objectives

The main aim of the therapeutic intervention is to change the negative perceptions that he now holds about himself in this domain-specific environment. Craig wants to feel confident once more in his abilities as a presenter both with small and large audiences, to have a clear mind and be succinct and inspiring and not have the constant worry of wondering whether another traumatic incident will occur.

Treatment plan: EMDR followed by CH

Research informs us that the process of replacing negative perceptions and thoughts with more rational ways of understanding problems allows individuals to reassess feared situations so that they become more manageable.[4] As there is no history of any previous trauma in the life of this patient the main focus of therapy will be the single traumatic experience aforementioned, initially concentrating on the feared situation. EMDR, through a process of desensitisation, is designed to change any dysfunctional cognitions and images linked to the disparate memory and this should enable Craig to look forward once more to forthcoming meetings rather than dreading them. Hypnosis can then be applied as an adjunct to EMDR. The process of hypnosis enhances the effectiveness of therapy and creates the belief of self-efficacy. When used as an adjunct to a particular form of therapy, whether behavioural, cognitive, or cognitive behavioural, the effects can enhance the treatment outcome.[5] Post-hypnotic suggestions given during hypnotherapy are also an important part of the therapy and are used to shape desired future behaviour. In fact it has been argued that it can be powerful in altering problem behaviours, dysfunctional cognitions and negative behaviours.[6] By use of both therapies, EMDR and hypnotherapy, the efficacy of treatment should be strengthened and enhanced.

First treatment (EMDR): 12 March 2011

Before the onset of therapy Craig appeared responsive, although he was somewhat hesitant in relating his narrative. The narrative gives the opportunity of emotional release and catharsis in a safe environment, and allows the patient to express feelings openly by relating the story of a trauma, and this in itself can facilitate a process of desensitisation. However, before this process can begin a rapport needs to be established between the patient and therapist if the optimum therapeutic results are to be achieved. It is understood that careful listening to the patient's narrative helps to convey the therapist's sincere desire to help and facilitates a positive relationship.[7] As the narrative progressed Craig seemed uncomfortable and embarrassed when relating the trauma he had experienced in the workplace. It was clearly producing an anxiety response as he felt (when relating the incident) that he was 'going into panic mode'.

This incident clearly needs to be re-examined to enable a process of desensitisation of the negative cognitions and memories. Craig already had some knowledge of the process and protocols of EMDR and was happy to embark on this treatment. The trauma target was the meeting, which Craig rated as an 8 on the SUD scale. His negative cognitions were feelings of being pathetic, shock, helplessness and disbelief. He felt that he had let himself down and the main emotion was one of embarrassment. As the therapy progressed, gradually his subjective SUD rating lowered to a 0, the lowest level of disturbance (this took approximately 30 minutes). At this point, in discussion his perceptions had changed and his understanding of exactly why this had happened to him became clear. He could see that a lack of preparation was key to his negative experience. He now held positive cognitions regarding similar forthcoming situations where his aim was to be 'succinct, clear in his mind, confident and inspiring'. He rated his self-belief in these things between a 5 and a 6, the highest level of positive cognition being 7. This first appointment took one hour 15 minutes. The second appointment was booked for the following week.

Second treatment (CH): 19 March 2011

In therapy Craig reported that he had felt much happier at work and that he had not been worrying over future meetings. This second session (of one hour duration) was designed to reinforce and intensify the cognitive restructuring achieved in the first session. It was directed at positive imagery, goal-setting and organisational skills in the workplace. Of greatest importance to Craig was his need for disciplined preparation, not only in the content of his spoken text at meetings but also in being prepared for any questions that might arise.

Before induction, as this was his first experience of hypnosis, it was explained that trance is a natural state of mind which is entered into without realising – as in day-dreaming. It is believed that hypnosis is the process of communication with the unconscious mind enabling an unconscious response to suggestion.[8] Craig chose three key words regarding his work which he felt would cover day-to-day responsibilities, small meetings and larger presentations: *confident, prepared* and *succinct*. These words would be spoken by the therapist at key points during therapy and anchored by touch on the patient's dominant wrist. In hypnosis some patients are able to relax fully which enables a deeper trance-like state, and this was the case with Craig. Positive suggestions and positive imagery of different subjective aspects of his work were given to create and strengthen his belief of self-efficacy. In fact a trance-state has been described as a special psychological state in which patients can re-associate and reorganise their inner psychological complexities when the critical faculty of the mind is bypassed, enabling the processing of thoughts in the unconscious mind to be transferred to the conscious in the waking state.[9] At the end of the session Craig described feeling 'freer and lighter' and was looking forward to the challenges of work. He had a meeting the following week to which he was now looking forward. A further session was not booked.

Craig's self-assessment of treatment

I was suffering badly at work from what I now realise was performance anxiety. This had come on suddenly after a catastrophic meeting at work where I felt I let myself down badly. Up until this point I had always felt confident that I could hold my own in meetings and I had also enjoyed giving presentations. After this meeting I was very worried that if this happened once it could happen again. I started looking at different therapies that were out there and decided to try hypnotherapy as this appeared to be a quick acting therapy as I had more meetings and presentations on the horizon that I was really worried about. After the first session (which turned out to be EMDR) I certainly felt much better about myself, and when thinking about forthcoming situations where I felt I would be on show I didn't feel nearly as anxious. It was strange, I just felt much calmer about everything. The second session was hypnotherapy which I found really relaxing. The session focused on my work, on the things which were most important to me, focusing on positive imaging. At the end of the session I felt that I could go into those meetings with my old confidence, knowing exactly what I had to do and preparing thoroughly, and funnily enough I looked forward to the first meeting which was within a few days. On the morning of the meeting I had a little twinge of anxiety but as soon as I walked into the room I was fine and knew that I could do a good job. I didn't lose my train of thought like last time, felt that I was imparting my knowledge and that they were listening and even managed to deal with some of the tricky questions that can arise in these meetings. In short I felt good about myself and that I had done a good job. The joint treatments that I had received were very effective for me. I understand that I was a good subject for trance induction which I think made the treatment for me even better.

(Written report, May 2011)

Therapist's objective assessment of treatment

Craig contacted me shortly after his next meeting at work. He had felt positive, confident and that he had done a good job. The joint interventions of EMDR and hypnotherapy appear to have achieved the desired outcome. It could be said that hypnotherapy alone might also have produced the same result. However by the use of EMDR as the initial treatment the desensitisation process of negativity which this patient held regarding the trauma experienced in the work place was reduced to the lowest level on the SUD scale. This would facilitate and enhance the process of hypnotherapy in strengthening positive suggestions, positive imagery and ego-strengthening. In fact it is argued that positive suggestions given in trance, when repeated sufficiently, become embedded in the unconscious mind to be acted upon in the conscious state.[10,11] It has further been argued that hypnosis breaks through the limitations of conscious attitudes and frees the unconscious potential for problem solving;[9] also that it facilitates divergent thinking, maximising awareness, attentional focus and concentration.[12]

Researcher's reflections on treatment suitability

It could be argued that a number of different therapies would have had the same beneficial effect in this case but it could also further be argued that a resolution to the problem would not have been achieved in only two sessions of such therapies. Psychopathological conditions such as anxiety disorders are usually treated by mainstream cognitive-behavioural approaches; however, recent literature suggests that these therapies may have their limitations and may have unintended unfavourable consequences such that the original presenting symptoms are weakened but may be replaced by other uncomfortable symptoms.[13] The intricate balance between cognitive, physiological and emotional states has been highlighted through research conducted into cognitive perceptions and their effect on physiological functions such as heart regulation.[14,15]

In the search for effective cures for the reduction of anxiety in performance, as well as the cognitive behavioural therapies, meditative interventions (meditation and yoga) are now being used for the reduction of anxiety. Meditation has its roots in the Buddhist tradition in India and is associated with decreases in stress and anxiety.[16] Research has found that the specific techniques used in meditation are effective for the reduction of stress, and that meditation produces decrements in trait levels of anxiety (an individual's general level of anxiety) through lower autonomic arousal.[17] This research was extended through longitudinal monitoring of the physical effect of meditation on the brain which demonstrated that left-sided anterior activation in the brain is increased by long-term meditation, a pattern that has been previously associated with positive affect.[18] The literature has shown that mindfulness meditation is a unique form of consciousness and is not merely a degree of a state of relaxation.[19] It has been described as a mode of mental functioning, the ability to step out of conceptual limitations, identify new solutions and give added insight.[20] Most types of meditation involve techniques which focus attention on an image, a word or a phrase, or controlled breathing.

In 2004 a group of behavioural scientists proposed a two-component model of mindfulness/meditation involving the self-regulation of attention allowing focus on the immediate experience, together with the adoption of certain perceptions of the experience characterised by curiosity, openness and acceptance.[21] Extending this research by the use of magnetic resonance imaging scans on subjects who have practised the techniques long-term, investigations have shown that mindfulness might be associated with changes in the brain's physical structure.[22] Currently ancient meditation practice has been integrated with modern psychotherapeutic techniques such as dialectical behavioural therapy and mindfulness-based cognitive therapy used in Chan meditation.[23] The benefits of practising meditation/ mindfulness for the reduction of anxiety cannot be doubted; however the limitations would appear to be the long-term nature of the intervention before a beneficial effect is achieved requiring a long-term learning programme (six months plus). In the case presented here the patient required a changed behaviour as quickly as possible for his acute performance anxiety. The multimodal interventions administered in two sessions of therapy gave a quick acting positive result.

Longitudinal outcome: September 2011

Craig contacted me six months post-therapy as requested, so that the longitudinal effect of therapy could be ascertained. He felt that he had maintained the positive cognitive effect both in small meetings and in larger presentations, although occasionally he could still feel apprehensive and nervous. However he felt the thorough preparation which he was still maintaining enabled him to remain clear-headed and calm when situations became tricky so that he no longer had the former panic that he had experienced pre-therapy. At this time he felt no need for any further therapy.

References

1 Hardy, L., Beattie, S., & Woodman, T. (2007). Anxiety-induced performance catastrophes: Investigating effort required as an asymmetry factor. *British Journal of Psychology*, *98*(1), 15–31.

2 Eysenck, M.W. (1997). *Anxiety and cognition: A unified theory*. Hove: Psychology Press.

3 Steptoe, A. (2001). Negative emotions in music making: The problem of performance anxiety. In P.N. Juslin & J.A. Sloboda (eds), *Music and emotion: Theory and research* (pp. 291–307). Oxford: Oxford University Press.

4 Beck, A.T. (1964). Thinking and depression. Part II: Theory and therapy. *Archives of General Psychiatry*, *9*, 324–333.

5 Brown, D.P., & Fromm, E. (1986). *Hypnotherapy and behavioral medicine*. Hillsdale, NJ: Lawrence Erlbaum.

6 Barrios, A.A. (1973). Posthypnotic suggestion in high-order conditioning: A methodological and experimental analysis. *International Journal of Clinical and Experimental Hypnosis*, *21*, 32–50.

7 Garfield, S.L. (2003). Eclectic psychotherapy: A common factors approach. In J.C. Norcross & M.R. Goldfried (eds), *Handbook of psychotherapy integration* (pp. 169–201). New York: Oxford University Press.

8 Barnett, E.A. (1989). *Analytical hypnotherapy: Principles and practice*. Glendale, CA: Westwood Publishing.

9 Rossi, E.L., & Cheek, D.B. (1994). *Mind-body therapy: Methods of ideodynamic healing in hypnosis*. New York: W.W. Norton.

10 Heap, M., & Aravind, K.K. (2002). *Hartland's medical and dental hypnosis* (4th edn). London: Churchill Livingstone.

11 Alladin, A. (2008). *Cognitive hypnotherapy: An integrated approach to the treatment of emotional disorders*. Chichester: John Wiley & Sons.

12 Tosi, D.J., & Baisden, B.S. (1984). Cognitive-experiential therapy and hypnosis. In W.C. Wester & A.H. Smith (eds), *Clinical hypnosis: A multidisciplinary approach* (pp. 155–178). Philadelphia, PA: J.B. Lippincott.

13 Roemer, L., & Orsillo, S.M. (2002). Expanding our conceptualization of and treatment for generalized anxiety disorder: Integrating mindfulness/acceptance-based approaches with existing cognitive-behavioral models. *Clinical Psychology: Science and Practice*, *9*(1), 54–68.

14 McCraty, R. (2003a). *Heart-brain neurodynamics: The making of emotions*. Boulder Creek, CA: HeartMath Research Center.

15 McCraty, R. (2003b). *The scientific role of the heart in learning and performance*. Boulder Creek, CA: HeartMath Research Center.

16 Kemper, K.J., & Shannon, S. (2007). Complementary and alternative medicine therapies to promote healthy moods. *Pediatric Clinics of North America*, *54*(6), 901–926.

17 Davidson, R.J., Goleman, D.J., & Schwartz, G.E. (1976). Attentional and affective concomitants of meditation: A cross-sectional study. *Journal of Abnormal Psychology, 85*(2), 235–238.

18 Davidson, R.J., Kabat-Zinn, J., Schumacher, J., Rosenkrantz, M., Muller, D., & Santorelli, S.F. (2003). Alterations in brain and immune function produced by mindfulness meditation. *Psychosomatic Medicine, 65*, 564–570.

19 Dunn, B.R., Hartigan J.A., & Mikulas, W.L. (1999). Concentration and mindfulness meditation: Unique forms of consciousness? *Applied Psychophysiology and Biofeedback, 24*(3), 147–165.

20 Kutz, I., Borysenko, J.Z., & Benson, H. (1985). Meditation and psychotherapy: A rationale for the integration of dynamic psychotherapy, the relaxation response, and mindfulness meditation. *American Journal of Psychiatry, 142*(1), 1–8.

21 Bishop, R.S., Lau, M., Shapiro, S., Carlson, L., Anderson, N.D., Carmody, J., et al. (2004). Mindfulness: A proposed operational definition. *Clinical Psychology: Science and Practice, 11*(3), 230–241.

22 Lazar, S.W., Kerr, C.E., Wasserman, R.H., Gray, J.R., Greve, D.N., Treadway, M.T., et al. (2005). Meditation experience is associated with increased cortical thickness. *Neuroreport, 16*(17), 1893–1897.

23 Lin, P., Chang, J., Zemon, V., & Midlarsky, E. (2008). Silent illumination: A study on Chan (Zen) meditation, anxiety, and musical performance quality. *Psychology of Music, 36*(2), 139–155.

13 Presentations no longer feared post-therapy

An exciting experience

Identifying information

Name:	Margaret
Anxiety in the work place:	Presentations
Gender:	Female
Age:	43 years
Occupation:	Manager of a small information technology company
Referral:	Recommendation

Case history: Margaret's narrative

I run my own small company which I have done for the last 15 years; it is like a family business. I love my job, in fact I'm passionate about it, I love helping people and showing them the latest technological software. However I have been noticing that I am becoming really anxious during presentations, which is an important part of my work. I don't start to worry days before the presentation as I prepare well and know exactly how I want the presentation to go, it seems to be minutes before it starts I get different physical symptoms. My hands start to shake, and my stomach begins churning. When I start speaking my voice shakes and I can't seem to control my movements, I lose focus and go blank and my mouth feels really dry. I just feel tense all over but especially in my shoulders. I didn't know what was happening the first time my mouth went dry and my voice started to shake and this made me feel really anxious. When I was a teenager I did conference presentations and I presented at exhibitions, and had no symptoms then no matter how large the audience. I don't know why this is happening now but it's really distressing me and I would love to get back to how I was years ago.

Case formulation

Therapist's interpretation of Margaret's narrative

Margaret appears to be a classic case of an individual suffering from performance anxiety. She describes how she is passionate about her job, and loves introducing the latest software. However, she has become overly anxious in presentations where she experiences both cognitive and acute physiological anxiety experiencing crippling somatic symptoms. She is not overly anxious in the days prior to the presentation but suffers acute cognitive anxiety as she crosses the threshold minutes before she begins. This can be contrasted with her description of the presentations she gave in her youth. Margaret has no recollection of any specific incidents which may have triggered the uncomfortable and distressing symptoms which she is now experiencing.

Critical analysis: therapist

It is thought that performance anxiety lies within the broad domain of social anxiety, which occurs when psychological discomfort in situation-dependent states leads to anxiety.[1] However it is a temporary condition and changes according to the environmental situations and pressures and the degree of threat perceived by the individual.[2] This condition can also be thought of as state anxiety (see Chapter 1, p. 4) and has been described as perceived feelings of apprehension and tension accompanied by the activation of arousal in specific situations.[3] A strong relationship between state anxiety and psychological discomfort in situation-dependent states has been reported in the literature,[4] and is thought to develop through an interaction of genetic factors, innate temperament, parental influences, conditioning events and cognitive influences.[5] Experienced, accomplished artists in the fields of music and acting, and in non-artistic performances such as sport, public speaking, oral examinations and presentations, can develop performance anxiety. The individual's perception of the demand can determine the outcome, whether the experience is positive or negative.[6]

An analysis of Margaret's narration suggests that she is suffering from a form of focal anxiety. She experiences this in one specific situation only and has no wider problems in other areas of work or social activities. It appears that performance anxiety has been generated from the time the distressing physiological/somatic symptoms of anxiety were first experienced during a presentation. When anticipating a similar situation she now has negative perceptions regarding the recurrence of her symptoms. It has been suggested that negative cognitions operating in feared situations include fear of negative evaluation, self-consciousness, self-deprecating thoughts and self-blaming attributions for difficulties, resulting in heightened physiological activity.[4]

Margaret displays the typical symptoms of 'how the mind affects the body'. In therapy she presented with the following negative cognitions/emotions and somatic symptoms regarding her presentations (direct quotes):

Negative thoughts

'I'm disappointed with myself'

'I could do better'

'I'm restricted'.

Emotions experienced were:

fear; and

anger.

Somatic symptoms experienced during the presentation were:

shaking of body/voice;

dry mouth;

stomach churning;

sweaty;

tension in neck; and

legs feeling weak.

Aims and objectives

The aim of the therapy is to change the subjective negative perceptions and responses regarding her presentations, so that she longer feels threatened in performance. A further aim is to reduce the fear to a controllable level, so that her arousal level is comfortable for her. The main objective is that she can give her optimum level of performance without experiencing the extremely uncomfortable somatic symptoms which are exacerbating the anxiety, so that she is able to feel confident and in control of the situation.

Treatment plan: EMDR and CH

This is a somewhat unusual case as there does not appear to be a specific trigger which instigated the acute anxiety experienced at the presentations.

A diagnostic treatment would suggest that hypnotherapy alone would be an effective therapy as the unconscious mind cannot distinguish between a real threat and a perceived threat. The important elements are to unlearn the negative responses, and this is best achieved through hypnosis, as hypnotherapy helps to reframe the thinking and enables the appropriate positive perceptions to be reinstated. In fact it has been argued that by accessing the unconscious mind during trance state, hypnotic suggestions can aid the innate tendency of the mind to heal itself and can produce profound changes in the reported experience.[7]

Before the commencement of treatment, however, Margaret rated her experience of fear and discomfort at presentations as 9 on the SUD scale where 10 is the highest level. It was therefore decided by the therapist that the strongest treatment giving the most beneficial results would be a multi-modal treatment of EMDR followed by hypnotherapy. EMDR identifies the stressors and enables desensitisation and dissociation from them. Investigations have found that EMDR aids emotional adjustment (through neuro-entrainment); it develops emotional control which involves at least four essential factors:[8]

a)   the ability to identify one's own emotional state and the state of others;
b)   the ability to understand the natural course of emotions;
c)   the ability to reason and argue about one's own emotions and the emotions of others; and
d)   the ability to deal with and control subjective emotions.

First treatment (EMDR): 16 March 2015

Margaret related her narrative, during which time she seemed nervous and tense as she explained that her next presentation, a really important award ceremony, was only two weeks away, and she was anxious not to have a recurrence of her previous somatic symptoms. The process of EMDR, and the reason for this treatment being given as the initial therapy, was first explained to Margaret, who was happy to proceed. This first treatment lasted for one hour and 30 minutes.

The initial target (the worst experience) was the first presentation when she had experienced the distressing somatic symptoms. The rating on the SUD scale (as stated above) was 9, indicating high trauma (almost the top of the scale). The primary negative cognition that she held about herself when thinking of this incident was one of disappointment and that she could do much better; however interestingly she felt that she had to be perfect and that she had fallen far short of her own expectations. Her ideal state for future performances was that 'I'm not limited by this past experience and that I can give confident performances and know that it won't happen again'. However when asked how truly she believed these positive statements, her rating on the validity of cognition (VOC) scale was 3 where the top of the scale is 7.

At the start of treatment the main emotion was of fear, and when imagining being in this situation *in vivo* from the safety of the therapy room her stomach began churning and she felt tension in the back of the neck. As the treatment proceeded and the initial trauma was desensitised her rating on the SUD dropped to a level 1 (almost the bottom of the scale). Interestingly as the rating on the SUD was gradually decreasing so the tension in her neck began moving down her arm and at 1 was gone, so that there was no longer any tension in either the neck or arm. It was as if once her mind had reprocessed the memory, her body no longer needed the accompanying somatic symptom and this could be released. This is an interesting phenomenon. In fact it has been argued that when the patient is confronted with the negative situation and learns that it can be faced without any catastrophic consequences, this can produce positive results, both cognitive and physiological.[9] Checking the VOC at the end of the session (her belief in the positive cognitions, how she wanted to be in presentations) this had risen to a 7, the top of the VOC scale and her main thoughts were 'I know that it won't happen again' and 'I don't have to be perfect, I can allow myself to make small slips and still give a very good presentation'. There is an old Chinese proverb: 'Go to the heart of danger, for there you will find safety.'

Second treatment (CH): 23 March 2015

Margaret reported feeling good regarding the forthcoming presentation which was now only five days away and was looking forward to the hypnotherapy session. The experience of hypnosis was explained although she already had knowledge of the process as I had previously treated her daughter. Before going into the trance state she chose three key words to enhance her performance, *positive*, *excited* and *focused*, as this is how she imagined herself being in performance. The hypnotherapy session lasted for one hour, and was focused on goal setting and visualisation, beginning with her past experiences as a teenager where she held positive cognitions in her abilities as an inspiring, confident presenter who enjoyed reaching goals and improving. This positive imagery was then transposed to the present time and the forthcoming presentation, seeing herself just as she wanted to be, prior to, during and post-presentation and anchoring her key words to reinforce the positivity. At the end of the session she was looking forward to the presentation instead of dreading it.

Margaret's assessment of treatment

> I had two therapy sessions and during that time I was taken through a meditation-type procedure which helped me recognise and feel the emotions that take over when I am giving a presentation. During the treatments instead of the fear consuming me I was able to acknowledge it and to let it go. The techniques and key words that I was given in therapy to use if I felt 'at all wobbly' had been 'positive', 'excited' and 'focused', using anchor points on my wrist to help with any physical feelings during the presentation; I felt that this also gave me added confidence. I am so pleased as before this treatment of only two therapies just the thought of what I had to do petrified me. They have made such a difference to the way I feel about giving presentations and doing any public speaking.
>
> (Testimonial, April 2015)

Therapist's assessment of treatment

In therapy the maladaptive cognitions and behaviours that this patient was experiencing in a performance situation were identified and targeted. There were six different somatic symptoms (see above). The experience of having a dry mouth and a shaking voice while giving an oral presentation can be particularly distressful. In fact it has been argued that somatic symptoms tend to perpetuate and reinforce anxiety and when a speaker exhibits these symptoms this can elicit a negative reaction from an audience, fulfilling the performer's pessimistic expectations.[10] Note that she felt that she had to be perfect in performance and was falling short of her own expectations. In the therapist's opinion this aspect of her personality was exacerbating her anxiety.

Socially prescribed perfectionism is most strongly associated with fear of negative evaluation, as it is associated with the imagery of an evaluating, disapproving other.[11] In fact it is believed that aspects of perfectionism associated with performance can include a higher anxiety level and an expected failure orientation in performance.[12] It has been found that one of the components of perfectionism is the need to present a flawless image to others, and this has been significantly associated with anxiety sensitivity.[13] At the end of the first session (EMDR), Margaret's perceptions had changed: 'I don't have to be perfect, I can allow myself to make small slips and still give a very good presentation.' The multi-modal therapy adopted in this case appears to have exerted a positive effect on performance outcome enabling attainment of her optimum performance level. The negative cognitions and emotions which she held pre-therapy were changed in two sessions giving positive behavioural outcomes so that she is able to look forward, feel confident and excited about forthcoming presentations.

Researcher's reflections on treatment suitability

Cognitive distortions that underlie performance anxiety have been categorised as follows:[10]

overestimating threat;

underestimating own competence;

selective attention to own arousal or to others' negative responses; and

negative pessimistic self-talk.

The diagnostic classification for performance anxiety may vary with each individual, and treatment should be varied accordingly. The case study cited here successfully addressed the four categories listed above through a combination of EMDR and hypnotherapy; however other treatments being offered could affect a similar positive outcome for this condition.

It has been shown that cognitive behavioural therapy (CBT), with components of exposure and retraining, can ameliorate performance anxiety,[14,15] and for those individuals who wish to be more pro-active in their own self-treatment of performance anxiety CBT may offer an effective alternative. It teaches the recognition of pessimistic thoughts pre-, during and post-performance, and replaces negativity with rational helpful thoughts based on the assimilated information.[16]

Exposure therapy is another approach used to alleviate performance anxiety to help individuals face feared situations (see Chapter 8, p. 76). Strategies employed include imagination, role play, confrontation, video recording and homework assignments.[16] One of the first published studies using an exposure-based behavioural approach found that this therapy reduced self-reported anxiety and performance errors in piano recitals more than in the control condition.[17] Exposure *in vivo* creates desensitisation; confronting the feared object or situation reduces the fear so that this is managed or reduced in subsequent exposures. It can be argued that EMDR may be a variant on standard exposure treatments.[18] While desensitisation therapies can follow different procedures, the basic principles of exposure to the feared situation are always applied but can be delivered in different formats.

Neuro-linguisitic programming (NLP) uses techniques and procedures of systematic desensitisation of a feared or traumatic experience (see Chapter 5,

p. 48). It moves through three different stages of imagining the situation/experience as on a cinema screen. Stage 1 creates distance from the experience so that the individual is not physically or mentally overwhelmed. In Stage 2 exposure is increased as the subject imagines moving closer to the screen. At Stage 3 the experience is pictured as being quickly rewound. This has the effect of re-imprinting the traumatic memory in a different way (running the film backwards); it has been suggested that this scrambles the information which was imprinted at the time of the trauma so that in this form it no longer makes sense and loses its power.[19]

Both EMDR and hypnotherapy use a process of desensitisation to moderate dysfunctional memories that may be held of past or present emotional trauma. The principles of EMDR use virtual experience to desensitise trauma. During treatment the individual imagines a past traumatic situation and revisits from a safe place the emotions, body sensations and negative cognitions experienced at that time. Research informs us that through this process the past trauma is gradually desensitised.[20] Hypnotherapy also uses desensitisation to moderate emotional experiences. While the patient is in a trance-like state (and this can be a self-induced trance which can be taught during hypnotherapy), fully relaxed with no bodily tension, the feared situation can be imagined and confronted. Positive ideas, thoughts and feelings are introduced enabling cognitive and emotional re-experiencing of the former uncomfortable situation.

Physiological therapies and therapies controlling physical functions are also being offered for the management of performance anxiety including bio-feedback, cognitive imagery, the Alexander Technique, yoga and relaxation techniques. Relaxation training is aimed at helping individuals recognise and respond to physical arousal during performance where progressive muscle relaxation is practised first in session and then as homework.[16] Social/mental skills training is another approach adopted for this condition, where more appropriate behaviours in performance are looked at in session, including modelling, behaviour rehearsal, corrective feedback and homework assignments such as video recording performances.[16,21]

Pharmacological interventions are also used to treat performance anxiety; the most common choices are short-acting agents such as beta blockers. These can relieve hyper-arousal and somatic symptoms such as tachycardia, tremor in body and voice when used in low doses for mild to moderate performance anxiety.[22] However, although medication can help diminish physical symptoms of anxiety, individuals may develop psychological dependency and feel unable to perform without these drugs.

Although the therapies discussed here can have positive effects on performance anxiety the drawback is the longitudinal nature of the treatments, some taking six months or more. In comparison, EMDR and hypnotherapy are psychodynamic therapies which achieve positive clinical effects in a short space of time without the need for homework (CBT) or prolonged focus as used in exposure therapies or the physiological therapies. A multimodal approach, as adopted in this case using CH as an adjunct to EMDR, addresses behaviour, affect, sensation and imagery, and a positive result was achieved in two sessions only. It could be argued that a drawback to the other therapies is the number of sessions required to affect a positive change in behaviour.

Longitudinal outcome

Margaret emailed me a few days after her presentation:

> I was overjoyed on the evening because I delivered my speech calmly, professionally and I was in control. It gave me such a buzz, I even added in 'off the cuff' sentences which complemented my speech, and I felt so elated when returning to my seat. It was amazing because the feedback was so wonderful.

She is now preparing her speech for the coming year and feels that there is no need to worry at all about delivering it: 'I now just have to make sure that I do not get carried away and talk for too long!!'

References

1 Crozier, W.R., & Alden, L.E. (2005). Constructs of social anxiety. In W.R. Crozier & L. E. Alden (eds), *Social anxiety for clinicians: The essential handbook* (pp. 1–26). Chichester: John Wiley & Sons.

2 Spielberger, C.D. (1972). Anxiety as an emotional state. In C.D. Spielberger (ed.), *Anxiety: Current trends in theory and research* (pp. 23–49). New York: Academic Press.

3 Spielberger, C.D. (1966). Theory and research on anxiety. In C.D. Spielberger (ed.), *Anxiety and behaviour* (pp. 4–22). London: Academic Press.

4 Turner, S.M., Beidel, D.C., & Townsley, R.M. (1990). Social phobia: Relationship to shyness. *Behaviour Research and Therapy, 2*, 497–505.

5 Ollendick, T.H., & Hirshfeld-Becker, D.R. (2002). The developmental psychopathology of social anxiety disorder. *Biological Psychiatry, 51*(1), 44–58.

6 Beatty, M. (1998). Situational and predispositional correlates of public speaking anxiety. *Communication Education, 37*, 28–39.

7 Erickson, M.H., & Rossi, E. (1974). Varieties of hypnotic amnesia. *American Journal of Clinical Hypnosis, 17*, 143–157.

8 Servan-Schreiber, D. (2003). *Guérir le Stress, l'Anxiété et la Dépression sans Médicaments ni Psychanalyse*. Paris: Robert Laffont.

9 Norcross, J.C., & Goldfried, M.R. (eds) (2005). *Handbook of psychotherapy integration* (2nd edn). New York: Oxford.

10 Kelly, V.C., & Saveanu, R.V. (2005). Performance anxiety: How to ease stage fright. *Current Psychiatry 4*(6), 25–34.

11 Tangney, J.P. (2002). Perfectionism and the self-conscious emotions: Shame, guilt, embarrassment, and pride. In G.L. Flett & P.L. Hewitt (eds), *Perfectionism: Theory, research, and treatment* (pp. 199–215). Washington, DC: American Psychological Association.

12 Hall, H.K., Kerr, A.W., & Matthews, J. (1998). Precompetitive anxiety in sport: The contribution of achievement goals and perfectionism. *Journal of Sport and Exercise Psychology, 20,* 77–90.

13 Hewitt, P.L., Flett, G.L., Sherry, S.B., Habke, A.M., Parkin, M., Lam, R.W., et al. (2003). The interpersonal expression of perfectionism: Perfectionistic self-presentation and psychological distress. *Journal of Personality and Social Psychology, 156*(8), 1237–1243.

14 Merritt, L., Richards, A., & Davis, P. (2001). Performance anxiety: Loss of the spoken edge. *Journal of Voice, 15*(2), 257–269.

15 Rodebaugh, T.L., & Chambless, D.L. (2004). Cognitive therapy for performance anxiety. *Journal of Clinical Psychology, 60*(8), 809–820.

16 Heimberg, R.G. (2002). Cognitive-behavioural therapy for social anxiety disorder: current status and future directions. *Biological Psychiatry, 51,* 101–108.

17 Appel, S.S. (1976). Modifying solo performance anxiety in adult pianists. *Journal of Music Therapy, 13*(1), 2–16.

18 McGlynn, F.D., & Lohr, J.M. (1998). Nonspecific factors in research on empirically supported treatments: Measurement and procedural controls. Paper presented at the Annual Convention of the Association for Advancement of Behavior Therapy, Washington, DC.

19 Buswell, D. (2006). *Performance strategies for musicians: How to overcome stage fright and performance anxiety and perform at your peak . . . using NLP and visualisation.* Stansted Abbotts: MX Publishing.

20 Shapiro, F., & Forrest, M.S. (1997). *EMDR: The breakthrough 'eye movement' therapy for overcoming anxiety, stress and trauma.* New York: Basic Books.

21 Connolly, C., & Williamon, A. (2004). Mental skills training. In A. Williamon (ed.), *Musical excellence: Strategies and techniques to enhance performance* (pp. 221–245). New York: Oxford University Press.

22 Blanco, C., Antia, S.X., & Liebowitz, M.R. (2002). Pharmacotherapy of social anxiety disorder. *Biological Psychiatry, 51,* 109–120.

14　Future directions
The future is not set in stone

The future is not set in stone, and even if it was, stone can be broken.
(Melanie Rawn)

This book was designed to highlight the condition of performance anxiety and has shown that it is far from straightforward. However, I hope that through the sensitive accounts of anxiety given in the case studies, the reader has a better understanding of how anxiety is generated, how this cycle can be broken, and so has been given more insight into the human psyche.

Part I of the book documented performance anxiety, how it manifests itself, what its causes may be and current treatments used. Two further chapters gave insights into the two psychodynamic therapies adopted in the case studies.

In Part II the case studies gave reconstruction of past experiences through subjective narrative and have allowed the reader to access the inside story of performance anxiety. We saw the important role that negative affectivity plays in three different performance domains and the need to implement therapies that target such negativity quickly and effectively. By this means performance need no longer be dreaded and can become an enjoyable experience.

Implications

Science is a continual investigative enquiry probing new ideas and thinking. The treatment of anxiety and performance anxiety should be an evolving process, not entrenched in archaic thinking but enabling open-mindedness in looking at innovative therapies. An important implication from the case studies is that dysfunctional conditions which are anxiety-based can be alleviated through cognitive hypnotherapy (CH) or eye movement desensitisation and reprocessing (EMDR) – or a combination of both therapies – after very few sessions. The subjective longitudinal monitoring of performance experience has strongly suggested that the beneficial effects from the therapies are long-lasting. We have seen that the psychological principles adopted through the therapies used can be implemented for the reduction of anxiety in any performance situation. However, it is important to examine the complexity of psychological disorders against the background of existing empirical treatments and comorbid conditions, as other therapies also have the potential to be effective (discussed in the case studies, Chapters 5–13). A further important consideration is that this therapeutic approach has broader implications, having applications in areas of clinical disorder where negative affectivity is the underlying problem.

The case studies give qualitative evidence for the effectiveness of both CH and EMDR for the reduction of cognitive anxiety in performance (after only one session in two instances; see Chapters 7 and 8). However there is still need for caution, matching therapy suitability to the individual. Therapies that target the unconscious mind might not be the preferred choice of therapy for some individuals, such as those who have an aversion to hypnosis or are suffering from focal anxiety where no deep-seated problems exist (see Chapter 6).

Recommendations

Many writers and clinicians advocate the importance of using effective treatments for a wide range of disorders; however there is little research which investigates the use of CH or EMDR for anxiety in the performance field. The case studies reported here suggest that the therapies have an important contribution to make to our understanding and treatment of the widespread problem of performance anxiety in any domain. The most crucial challenge arising in the existing literature, and in the medical practice in the treatment of this condition, is the emphasis placed on the conscious as opposed to the unconscious mind; this would appear to be hindering progress in working towards a more robust and radical solution to this condition. Where fundamental psychological problems exist, therapies that deal solely with the conscious mind are not effective in their outcomes for everyone; quick-acting psychodynamic therapies as used in the cases in this book give faster and longer-lasting results.

There is scepticism of psychodynamic therapies in various areas, including the medical profession and the general public. Greater understanding of the therapeutic procedures and protocols of CH and EMDR is needed, together with more empirical research providing evidence of their effectiveness which will help to increase the credibility of these therapies.

It could be said that a limitation of this research is the lack of a control group, and this is a valid point; however the author's quantitative research into music performance anxiety with use of a control group gave statistical scientific evidence for the beneficial effects of these therapies.[1] The cases described in this book give in-depth qualitative information on the debilitating experience of performance anxiety adding to previous investigations, however further research in the field is needed. The author hopes that this book will inspire such research into the effects of these psychodynamic therapies. Once their efficacy is established it will increase therapy utilisation not only for performance situations that are anxiety-based but also other disorders and conditions that have anxiety as the root cause. The beneficial quick-acting effects of these therapies suggest that both might, after further research, deserve inclusion in National Health Service thinking, and be given similar status and standing as CBT, the therapy currently advocated by the medical profession for anxiety-based conditions. Given the efficacy of CH and EMDR after very few sessions, comparisons with CBT should now be conducted and cost effectiveness assessed.

Understanding the therapies, and education in their principles and protocols, is the key to overcoming diffidence and lack of knowledge. One way to manage this would be through direct collaboration between researchers, medical practitioners and therapists, bringing these disciplines together and working towards a shared agenda. Greater exposure and awareness is required globally, in journal articles, associations/societies and publications that focus on performance, so that the knowledge of these therapies can be more easily accessed by those afflicted with performance anxiety.

Anxiety UK is a national registered charity formed over 45 years ago. It is a user-led organisation run by those with personal experience of anxiety, stress and anxiety-based depression. While they offer CBT, counselling, acupuncture and clinical hypnotherapy their available list of treatments would be enhanced by the inclusion of EMDR. The International Society for Mental Training and Excellence (ISMTE) founded in 1989 focuses on encouraging excellence in performance and in all human endeavours: sport, the performing arts, work, education, health and life. Societies such as this would benefit from the knowledge of CH and EMDR to enhance the mental skills programmes which they already offer.

Associations that highlight the physical and psychological challenges faced by musicians in performance include the International Society for the Study of Tension in Performance (ISSTP) and the British Association for Performing Arts Medicine (BAPAM). There are also publications for musicians/music teachers, such as the journals of the European Piano Teacher's Association (EPTA), and *Libretto*, the quarterly journal of the

Associated Board of the Royal Schools of Music. It would be good to see these associations and journals recognise the effectiveness of these therapies to bring them to the attention of a wider public.

If the above recommendations are implemented, therapeutic interventions that target the unconscious mind could be viewed with a different perception, and given the status that they deserve. The analytical procedures which govern CH and EMDR recognise that individuals are unconsciously bound to the past. It is only when these demons are addressed that the individual is unshackled and can respond to the present in a natural, appropriate and positive way. The experiences reported here are testaments to this philosophy. Science is a continual investigative process probing new ideas and thinking. The treatment of both anxiety per se and performance anxiety should be an evolving process enabling us to move forward, investigating innovative interventions with an open mind.

Reference

1 Brooker, E. (2018). Music performance anxiety: A clinical outcome study into the effects of cognitive hypnotherapy and eye movement desensitisation and reprocessing in advanced pianists. *Psychology of Music*, *46*(1), 107–124.

Index

Note: References in *italics* are to figures, those in **bold** to tables.

Printed in the United States
by Baker & Taylor Publisher Services